TRANSCENDENT LEADERSHIP

THE 8 DIMENSIONS OF AWAKENED LEADERSHIP PRACTICE

RICHARD C ANDERSON DMS BSC (JOINT HONS) MA

CARE ADVANCE LTD

PUBLISHING

First published by Care Advance Ltd 2021

www.awakeningcoaching.co.uk

awakeningcoachinguk@gmail.com

For distributor details and how to order, please visit the 'contact' section on our website.

Text copyright: Richard C Anderson 2020

ISBN: 9798590094455

All rights reserved. No part of this book may be reproduced in any manner without prior written permission from the publishers.

The rights of Richard C Anderson as author have been asserted in accordance with the Copyright, Designs and Patents Act 1988.

Cover Design: Richard C Anderson

Care Advance Ltd Publishing serves to contribute to the spiritual unfoldment of humanity on our planet and seeks to govern its business from a comprehensively ethical perspective.

Contents

Foreword by Rev Don MacGregor 7

Introduction 9

1. The First Dimension:
   Knowing (The Key to Transcendence) 26

2. The Second Dimension:
   Seeing (Revealing Your Mission) 44

3. The Third Dimension:
   Being (Becoming You) 67

4. The Fourth Dimension:
   Aligning (The Shift to Third Level) 104

5. The Fifth Dimension:
   Connecting (The Centrality of Love) 129

6. The Sixth Dimension: Creating
   (Opening to Infinite Possibility) 156

7. The Seventh Dimension:
   Doing (Manifesting) 179

8. The Eighth Dimension:
   Resting (The Mind-Spirit Energy Cycle) 222

Summary of the 8 dimensions of Transcendent Leadership 240

Postscript 242

Previous Titles by The Author

Mind-Spirit Detox : Reboot, reset and recharge with 40 beautiful practices to deepen your oneness with Spirit.

O Books

ISBN-13 : 978-1789040449

Foreword

There is much talk of 'Oneness' in the world today. The recent Covid 19 pandemic has brought an awareness that we are one humanity, susceptible to the same diseases, having the same feelings and grief at losing a loved one, interconnected in so many ways by economics, food distribution, power supplies, communications technology and much more. The environmental climate crisis has brought us to realise we are one interconnected whole with the biosphere of the planet on which we dwell, we are an integral micro part of it. Whilst it is good to see that dawning realisation, there is another level to reach before humanity can turn things around to make this planet sustainable and that is a spiritual awakening, or 'transcendence' as Richard Anderson describes it.

Down through the ages, in most religious and spiritual traditions, there have been those mystics and seers who have proclaimed that we are all one within the divine One Life. It now seems that science is moving towards that same understanding. At the level of energy and information, leading scientists are saying that the universe is a cosmic hologram, with information patterns repeated throughout, and that everything in the universe is interconnected at an informational level. That informational level some describe as consciousness, which they say is not something we have, but is what we are – and there is only one Consciousness. Hence spiritual and scientific understandings are beginning to converge. This is a step too far for much materialistic science and inevitable reactions will challenge this viewpoint for many years. Yet there are those who perceive it and work with it. Richard Anderson is one of these people.

He has combined his own experience and beliefs with his wide-ranging leadership skills to trace a pathway to the most effective leadership. This is via recognising our own abilities and talents in leadership, but then getting our own ego out of the way, allowing the energy of Source, God, Divinity, the Universe, to flow and bring abundance. He suggests that we need to wake up to the divinity within, to make the inward connection, but then move outward into the world with a new perspective of surrender to the flow of divine energy and abundance.

In leadership skills, he moves us from the Transactional level, to the Transformational, then to the Transcendent, which, speaking as a Christian priest, is exactly what Jesus tried to do with his followers, with limited success. For the most part, the Church got stuck at the transactional level, as have many other traditions. Richard has written a remarkably practical and grounded spiritual work on leadership, based in a broad spirituality that draws on various contemporary teachers and also on ancient perennial wisdom teachings.

When Richard first asked if I would write a foreword to his book, I feared it might be a quite heavy read – but I couldn't have been more wrong! It is entertaining, enlightening and gave me a few laughs on the way. I think you will enjoy it!

Revd. Don MacGregor BSc MA *(Author of "Blue Sky God: the Evolution of Science and Christianity" and "Christianity Expanding: Into Universal Spirituality")*

Introduction

transactional/transformational/transcendent. Definition:
tranˈsɛnd(ə)nt,ˌtrɑːnˈsɛnd(ə)nt/
adjective
1. 1. beyond or above the range of normal or physical human experience.
"the search for a transcendent level of knowledge"

Conventional wisdom is a disease that leaders are particularly susceptible to. It's a malady which limits ambitions, stifles creativity and which keeps people trapped in a cycle of hard work, mediocre results and often mind-numbing boredom. In short, it's the perfect antidote to life.

In terms of leadership theory, conventional wisdom says that there are two levels: Transactional Leadership (Level One) and Transformational Leadership (Level Two). That's it. Just two levels. But what if there is another level above these two? For years I was astonished that there should just be two levels. After all, in other organisational disciplines, there are so many more than two of anything. Consider that there are at least 6 'Ps' of marketing; 6 'Ps' of retailing, 6 stages in the selling process and so on. Surely, then, there are more than a mere two levels of leadership practice?!

Indeed, a radically different level of leadership is now emerging, a level that will challenge conventional wisdom, break through self-imposed limits of possibility, bring about new thinking, and shift from daily drudgery and stress into a whole new field of practice. This is a place of creativity, of results, of new thinking and disruptive innovation. Welcome to the Third Level - Transcendent Leadership, where the world of emergent understanding and evolving human consciousness shatters existing paradigms and buries the tyranny of moribund leadership theory that belongs in the last century.

Embedded within this book is a code which unlocks your true leadership potential, which will enable you to experience the preternatural magic of transcendence in your own leadership practice. Each dimension of this code when absorbed into your mind and applied through your practice, will radically shift you away from the everyday world that you currently experience.

The root of the word 'leadership' literally means to go forth, to cross a threshold, to cross over from one world to another one, and that is what I invite you to do as you absorb the eight-dimensional code which will open the door to your own transcendence as a leader.

The imperative to transcend has never been more pressing - the leadership challenge facing us today is perhaps greater than ever before, such is the connectivity, pace and disruption experienced by virtually every organisation on the planet in this present moment. If we allow leadership to remain stuck within an atavistic paradigm, then organisations will remain exactly where they already are, on the same side of the threshold, in the very same place in which they started. The self-imposed boundaries of conventional thinking will only ever produce conventional results. That's simply not going to cut it in today's world.

The good news is that I know of very few people that truly want themselves, their teams and their organisation to remain exactly where they currently are. So the challenge to you as a leader is this: absolutely demand through every level of your body and mind that you wish to transcend to a new level of possibility. Demand the dissolution of all limited thinking, all fear, all negative energy that diminishes your effectiveness as a leader. Leave behind any liability that is holding you back. Then let curiosity and openness fill the void left behind. This will give you the best possible start to moving beyond the place in which your practice currently resides.

As you prepare your heart and your mind to absorb the knowledge contained in this eight-part code, say to yourself, 'Now I remove all my fears and limits' - make it a firm demand of your mind for action. This is very important. A weak, flaccid request will elicit weak, flaccid outcomes for you.

The importance of preparing yourself in all seriousness to explore the various dimensions is not just around your own self-development. As a leader, it's not about you. It's never been about you. It's about the people that you lead and the goods and/or services that your organisation produces. You are in service to that, and the tools and knowledge that you currently have will be accelerated and improved by an order of magnitude if you move beyond your current limits and truly embody the emergent truth contained within this book.

Opening up to the level of the transcendent will take you far beyond old patterns of leadership that no longer serve, and that is why this book is such a big deal. All projects, all organisations, all teams, all endeavours, be them large or small, from NASA to the World Health Organisation to the corner shop – all require leadership. Just imagine how the world could change if all leaders in all of these organisations were able to access the tools and understanding of Transcendent Leadership. If all blocks to thinking were removed and infinite possibility and creativity flooded organisations big and small around the globe, then humanity as a whole would take a giant leap forward.

****

It's funny how unpredicted events can shock your mind-belief system into a complete reset. Those moments of revelation that knock you off the trajectory that you have been happily travelling along for years. Imagine an icy rock travelling in a straight line through interstellar space; nothing intersecting its route for aeons. And then suddenly, something hits it; sets it off on an altogether different course. That's what happened to me. That new course was set to shatter the beliefs that had boundaried my notions of what the upper levels of leadership practice looked like.

For decades I had trodden a fairly traditional path in my leadership career. A degree in Economics and Politics set me up for a brief sojourn with PWC as a trainee Chartered Accountant. I like numbers but wanted more creativity so I got onto the National Health Service Management Training Scheme at Kings Fund College, then in Bayswater, London. Whilst managing in a busy acute hospital in London, I completed my Masters in Management Studies then went on to various courses run out of government departments such as the Cabinet Office. Learning how to motivate, to plan, to assess risk, set Key Performance Indicators and so on was pretty engaging but was far from revolutionary. My initial roles combined the nitty-gritty of front-line health services management, managing the Emergency Department, Surgery, Orthopaedics and so on, with more corporate roles such as Head of Planning and Performance. I was pretty much stuck in the left-brain world of health economics, performance indicators, monitoring arrangements, risk management and governance. I learnt from some incredible people and amazing leaders in my time but at no point in my first two decades or so in leadership did I ever feel as if I had stumbled across anything especially groundbreaking.

Until that is, a moment around seven years ago when a few events came together to shift me from my cosy relationship with the accepted mechanics of management and leadership.

I had always had a curious but rather conservative mind. I had a set of pretty fixed beliefs, about both myself and the world around me. But then something occurred which made me begin to question everything I had stood for for over four decades. This is the moment when I was knocked off the trajectory.

We were spending Christmas with my in-laws in South America. It was summer in Paraguay, which meant temperatures into the mid 40s (that's over 110 degrees Fahrenheit) and heavy, thundery deluges. We were there for five long weeks. Let me tell you that Paraguay is a long way from anywhere. It is a landlocked country, deep in the heart of South America, boundaried by a sea of green on all sides. It is a place to go to lose yourself, to recreate yourself. It is a place to go and think and to discover.

In the week preceding our trip, we had watched the Matt Damon movie, 'Hereafter', which had piqued my interest in Near Death Experiences (NDEs). As a Christian of the evangelical wing of the church, I had been brought up within something of a straitjacket of belief. NDEs really didn't figure in the traditional canon, and I was sure that preachers would for whatever reason react unfavourably to any kind of an interest in them. But in the humidity and heat of the long Paraguayan summer, and being such a distance from the religious thought police back home, I started exploring this phenomena. What I discovered about NDEs is not especially important to this narrative, save to say that by taking the first tentative steps away from dogma-driven belief, I began to open a door in my mind. It was as if a trickle of energy-giving water first began to seep around the edges of the door, then the force of water became more and more powerful until the door broke away from its hinges. Then the entire walls came down, shattered by a deluge of new ideas and concepts.

I began to explore writers and academics at the leading edge of biological science, human evolution, spirituality and quantum physics such as Dr Ervin László, Robert Monroe, Eric Butterworth, Rupert Spira, Dr Rupert Sheldrake, Dr Bruce Lipton, Dr Joe Dispenza, Adyashanti, Krishnamurti, Robert Lanza, Steven Pinker and many others.

My life had been so dominated by the left brain and linear thought that this field of discovery truly shattered my world view and let light in to places in my belief system that had lain closed and dark for my whole life.

> "Ring the bells (ring the bells) that still can ring
> Forget your perfect offering
> There is a crack in everything (there is a crack in everything)
> That's how the light gets in"
> Leonard Cohen (taken from 'Anthem')

Thus I completed my training in coaching and mentorship through the Academy of Awakening Coaching (based in California). I then added Integral Theory training under Ken Wilber, became a Holy Fire Reiki practitioner, followed by further study under Otto Scharmer through the Presencing Institute at the Massachusetts Institute of Technology (MIT). In my own leadership practice, I began using some of the most advanced, leading edge techniques available anywhere. And in training with a world-wide student body, people from Australia to Holland, from Miami to Mexico, I witnessed leaders and entrepreneurs in organisations all over the globe transform in ways that I could hardly have ever imagined possible.

I increasingly adopted and adapted this knowledge and understanding into my own team as a senior manager in the field of health and social care. Thus a revolution was born, both for me as a leader and for my staff. This combination of advanced practice, surrender of ego, of 'small self', of opening to the world of creativity and expansive possibilities produced some remarkable results in my teams: the lowest sickness rates, lowest staff vacancy rates, highest morale, greatest efficiency, best outcomes, and staff and team awards at both local and national levels.

Whilst other parts of the public sector were drowning under a sea of regulation, stress, impossible targets and a negative vortex of poor staff morale, resignations, and vacant posts, in my team, we were absolutely flying, loving our jobs, balancing our lives and hitting every target without breaking sweat. In 2020, my team nominated me for my organisation's Exceptional Leadership Award, which I was humbled to then be awarded by my employer, a health service organisation in the UK, employing some 8,000 staff.

This book is a distillation of everything I have learnt along the way. Through contemplation, concentration, meditation and active reflection, I have uncovered eight dimensions of leadership practice. These dimensions effectively constitute a code which, when applied, will lead you to the unfoldment of your own revolutionary path into the emergent practice of Transcendent Leadership.

Michael Shinagel, Dean at Harvard University, states that there are over 15,000 books on leadership currently in print. In my experience, they generally travel along a horizontal plane of understanding and learning, sticking firmly to the known ground of reductionist, materialist, quantifiable social sciences and received wisdom. One could spend a lifetime reading such material and emerge more knowledgeable but no further advanced in practice.

This book is different. It leaves behind the horizontal plane of learning and takes the reader upwards on the vertical plane to reach the most evolved, newly emergent levels of leadership practice. You will make the shift from day to day routine and basic grind, towards one where you and your entire team or organisation feel as if you are being carried on a force greater than that which you have ever experienced before, opening yourself to new vistas of understanding. As a Transcendent Leader, you will shift from being a manager of the mundane into becoming an artist of infinite possibility. As the dimensions unfold, I will help you to incorporate many new tools and techniques in your leadership practice. There is a helpful summary of the main practices in each dimension at the end of each chapter. Here's a selection of some of the knowledge and skills that you will encounter along the way:

- Achieving the super-charged power of the flow state
- Experiencing 'downloads' of information and guidance
- Obtaining insights into the emergent future
- Shifting to a higher frequency of awareness
- The ability to transmit energy to your team
- Achieving deeper levels of cohesiveness within your team
- Being on fire for your mission
- Understanding how to channel and use subtle energies

The key mission of Transcendent Leadership is to bring consciousness into the field of leadership practice. Consciousness is the key to understanding why Level Three (Transcendent Leadership) is so totally different to Levels One and Two (Transactional and Transformational Leadership). Third Level practice moves beyond the small self to encapsulate divine, cosmic consciousness – shifting from small mind to Big Mind, from egoic understanding to unbounded consciousness.

If you have been developing and improving and refining your leadership practice for some time, but feel that you have hit a plateau, it's because you're probably stuck at the top of the second level (Transformational Leadership). If you are going round and round stuck in a cycle of objective setting, monitoring, emails, burnout and stress, it's probably worse – you may well be stuck in First Level.

So let me briefly set out the key stages of evolution in leadership practice below, because they are fundamental to everything I talk about in the book:

First Level: Transactional Leadership - This is the least sophisticated but the commonest form of leadership practice. It is based on Taylor's Scientific Management model, which is somewhat akin to Newtonian physics. The basic paradigm is that rules are set (Standard Operating Procedures and so on) and management is rewarded on how well they know and adhere to the rules. Rewards are based on safely doing what is cascaded down. The threat of punishment often lurks implicitly or explicitly for not meeting targets or adhering to policy. Motivation is provided by avoiding punishment or potential monetary reward. Innovation is frowned upon in many instances as it could prove risky and is seen as an anathema to good governance. Efficiency, safety and productivity is championed. Organisational culture is not to be questioned or developed.

Second Level: Transformational Leadership - This involves a large, but still limited and boundaried shift in thinking. It includes First Level activities, but with a sprinkling of change management added into the mix. Effort is still required by the 'hero' leader. However, this level seeks to be pro-active and in the main, new ideas are welcomed.

Third Level: Transcendent Leadership - This is revolutionary in its nature, because at Third Level, you shift beyond 'self'. Here you are tapping into subtle energies, the higher self; expanding your furthest possible reach. Energies are traveling through you, not coming *from* you. In the world of organisational and managerial thought, this level is so new and so extraordinary that it can be seen to be on a totally different plane. It is truly a different paradigm compared to the previous two levels.

To shift from Second Level to Third Level leadership practice, you need to break through a barrier of understanding and of being. In virtually all aspects of the Third Level, the level of transcendence, the power you will derive is not your own power. When we look at energy, judgement, intuition, communication, presence, purpose, strategy, planning, authenticity and so on, to move from second to Third Level requires a surrendering of self. You cannot even hope to get near Third Level in your own power. You will see leaders all around you struggling, working long hours, displaying signs of stress, looking tired. This is because they have hit the outer limits of possibility at second level. They are doing everything using their own personal reserves of energy and power, this being quite obviously finite in nature.

At Third Level, you move beyond 'self' and you open to the power of the Universe, 'Big Mind', 'Source', 'God'. Whatever you name it, the essence is that it is beyond *you*. At the same time, it is *within* you. It is the very stuff that you are made up of. In fact, you can pretty much obtain everything you need to at Third Level simply by opening up to a new understanding of what or who you already really are – the consciousness that resides at the heart of *you*. You will learn that when you raise your own quality of awareness or consciousness, you will see a corresponding increase in the quality and quantity of results of your team or organisation. Entire systems will shift in their collective consciousness as a result of the shift of *your* consciousness.

So open yourself up, be a channel for the Universe. One of the key messages of Transcendent Leadership is that your humanity will only take you so far. If you want more power, more charisma, more connection, more inspiration, these can only come from the world beyond the small 'self'. The eight dimensions of transcendence that form the chapters of this book are like doorways into this world. The first four are the foundational dimensions; the ones that once open stay open. The latter four are cyclical; you travel through them and with them continually on your journey.

These are doors like no other, however. They are not something that can be learned with the mind alone. They are virtual doors that enable you to awaken to your true self, to transcend the consciousness of the skin-covered ego and shift into unity consciousness, a world of infinite possibility and divine creativity.

This will be truly revolutionary and revelatory for many people. You will meet resistance from colleagues along the way. This is because for many leaders, their world view is on lock-down. They will dismiss this out of hand, saying that their 'me', the mechanistic body, the brain, their abilities, is all that exists. Their belief system is small, oppressive and constrictive. The materialist/reductionist world view will leave them stuck at first or second level for ever. The reality is that these people will almost certainly exist within your own team.

However, there is emerging evidence around 'movements', around tipping points, that means that you can forge ahead in your Third Level journey regardless and the sheer creativity and enthusiasm that will come flooding through you will almost certainly positively affect them. Yes, this level is infectious. In my own experience, I have seen time and time again how whole groups of people can get swept up in the Third Level. Then the leverage you have at your fingertips is powerful beyond belief, because you will have shifted from struggling in your own potential, leading people doing likewise, towards a whole team of people seemingly flying with extraordinary power and innovation, using very little of their own energies.

So the only real question I have to pose for you right now is, 'how far are you willing to go'? Do you genuinely want to be the best possible leader you can be, utilising the most advanced tools, operating at the leading edge of human evolution? If so, then read on and push forwards. Or rather, surrender and open yourself to going forwards. There should be little or no pushing from your own power and strength. That is because at the heart of most magnificent, paradigm-shifting truths, there nearly always lies a paradox. Truth and paradox are rarely separated.

Third Level leadership is such a momentous leap away from second level that more than a little nudge is required to get there. It is a little like a rocket craft achieving escape velocity. Once this speed (25,020 mph) is achieved, it enables the craft to enter a new dimension. It's like being in a different universe. No longer is the craft weighed down by the earth's gravitational field, it is free to effortlessly soar on to the stars.

So it can be for you, too. I have accumulated some 50,000 hours worth of practice in my profession as a general manager in health, which is five times the fabled 10,000 hours necessary to develop mastery of a subject or art form or practice. So in terms of my own power and abilities, they're pretty good. But all of the accumulated knowledge, skill and experience in the world will only make you a good Level Two practitioner.

To achieve the 'escape velocity' requires you to engage in a paradox. The paradox is this: you have to fully let your brilliance, your genius, shine. You have to be the best version possible of yourself, yet at the same time, you have to fully get out of the way. Do the former, and you'll just be a brilliant leader at Level Two. Add in the latter, and you achieve flow. You begin the process of surrender, of release of ego, and you allow the unbounded power of the Universe to channel through you. You become part of the divine flow of being.

Therefore in order to access this level, you have to humble yourself and know that the radical nature of Third Level cannot ever flow through you without your admitting that this will never be accessed from ego, from effort, from your own power. Seemingly magical things happen at Third Level but more of the same – more work, more hours, more effort – is just not going to make the monumental leap for you.

Hegel said that truth is found neither in the thesis nor the antithesis, but in an emergent synthesis which reconciles the two. In the same way, I am always on the look out for the magical product of a paradoxical pair. It's often powerful and surprising, because it does not originate in regurgitated thought. I was fortunate enough to attend Brian Eno's illustrated lecture in Sadler's Wells Theatre in London back in 1992. We in the audience only learnt the title of the lecture at the end, 'Perfume, Defence and David Bowie's Wedding'. I took no notes, but to this day, I remember clearly the narrative.

Eno used to obsessively catalogue smell. He did so only because nobody had really done it before, such is the empirical elusiveness of the exercise - the difficulty in connecting smell with words. Furthermore, cataloguing is a left brain activity and smell is located in the right brain *(Eno has always had a fascination with combining logic (left brain) with art and beauty (right brain))*. However, one of the most intriguing aspects of all of this for Eno was the resulting outcome of combining two smells. He said, for instance, that combining roses and honey resulted in a smell reminiscent of motor oil. And this is the power of the paradox. Bringing your ultimate best self and then opening this up and standing aside produces the most remarkable channelling of Spirit. That's the power you need to hit escape velocity to take you to Level Three.

To some, this is a leap of faith. Until you experience the awesome connection with all that is, of opening up as a channel of divine wisdom, you will never quite know just how different this feels to doing everything in your own power, using your own energy and effort and struggle and human wisdom. But it is this that will take you through to Level Three.

When I posed the question, 'how far are you willing to go?' this is what it is all about. Because if you are unwilling to effectively go all the way into orbit, then you will remain forever trapped at Level Two. If, however, you want to go all the way, then you necessarily have to open up to a power infinitely greater than that of your own ego, mind and body.

The code in this book outlines the territory, but your exact route will be yours and yours alone, so keep a notepad and open a channel to creative intuition on your path and importantly, consider journaling your thoughts and actions as you move through the dimensions.

The eight key dimensions which unlock the transcendent level are divided equally into two sections of four dimensions. Each dimension includes practices which enable you to understand and assimilate the fundamental knowledge that you need in order to make the shift to Level Three. As each dimension is a call to action for you (i.e. it is an active, not a passive process), each one is associated with a verb. As such, the foundational dimensions are:

- Knowing
- Seeing
- Being
- Aligning

When you have worked through these foundational dimensions, they are effectively downloaded and installed. These dimensions are psycho-active in nature - they will change you and change the structure of your inner operating system, i.e. your mind. As such, you only need to move your consciousness back to them from time to time, as once installed, they will be running forever. They are effectively breakthroughs in understanding of and locating of self.

The final half of the book, the last four dimensions, are cyclical in nature. Again, each dimension is connected with verbs, which are:
- Connecting
- Creating
- Doing
- Resting

These four dimensions are alive, as they are part of the human condition. They are the fundamental cycle of leadership, a flow of living and life-affirming circularity. As such, they contain understanding and practices that are continually regenerating – rising, falling, being still and refreshing.

Dimensions one to four will enable you to fully understand your own true nature as an awakened being, living out your highest purpose in the present moment here on planet earth. Dimensions five to eight will facilitate your being able to stand aside to allow the flow of the universe to supercharge and drive everything in your team and in your organisation.

Summary of Practices and Reflections:

- Remove all fears and limits   11

Chapter 1

The First Dimension: Knowing

The Key to Transcendence

And so to the first of the foundational dimensions, as we move our awareness away from day to day narrative and mundane concerns right down to the heart-centre of understanding. This is a dimensional shift from logical reason towards a more fundamental, intuitive understanding of ultimate truth.

The verb that I have associated with this chapter is 'knowing'. Knowledge of your true nature is a necessary pre-condition to transcend through and beyond the world of transaction, of form, of day to day 'doing'. Awakening to your true nature and knowledge of what that is, is the foundation of evolved leadership.

The Oxford Dictionary defines consciousness as, 'the state of being aware of and responsive to one's surroundings', and 'a person's awareness or perception of something'. For me, then, the Awakened Leader is somebody who is fully immersed in the knowledge and consciousness of who or what they are and what their highest purpose is in respect to the practice that they are leading. But this on its own is insufficient. The Awakened Leader transcends the notion of the 'small self', the talking and walking ego, and opens to their true divine nature, an awakened consciousness that is a part of and indivisible from cosmic consciousness. As such they utilise the full resources of the field of being from which their own consciousness arises.

How many people are fully awake to these aspects of leadership practice? If you were to ask a random selection of leaders if they fully understand and have knowledge of who or what they really are, how many coherent answers will you receive? The question then arises, if somebody doesn't fully understand who they are, how can they fully understand what they are doing?

Thus when we awaken to knowledge of self and of our mission, we transcend the small self, the egoic self, the false self, and open up to the connection between our own divinity and the divinity of all that is. In this way, emptiness becomes form; what was once merely a possibility becomes something manifest. Something comes from nothing. Hence when I use the term, 'Knowing' in the title of this chapter, I mean it in a sense that is at the outermost horizons of the term. It isn't the knowledge of facts repeated from a black-board, rather, it is the ultimate knowledge that comes from transcending the small self and connecting with the divine within and the divine without.

Let me bring you back down to earth and illustrate how this plays out in the nitty-gritty of front-line management. I am part of a regional network of leadership coaches and as such, I was coaching a senior professional from a neighbouring county a few years back. When I am coaching, I come with no agenda, just my ears, my curiosity and a kit-bag of tools and techniques which I use as my heart and inspiration guide me. I open my awareness and ability to connect with subtle energies and I allow the wisdom of the universe to flow through me. So it was on this occasion.

The professional talked to me about a situation in which she had experienced conflict and trust issues in the past with a colleague. The problem was that the colleague in question was about to become her line-manager. She spent some ten minutes explaining the situation to me, including all of the history leading up to the current day. When I am coaching, I move (indeed, 'transcend') ordinary active listening. I listen with all of me, all of my body and all of my feelings. Paradoxically, the narrative is not actually very important to me *per se*. Whilst I'm listening, I am feeling into the contractions; the things that are said that trigger something in me. These are the things that we need to work on together in the session. On this occasion, the spark for me revolved around the egoic response of my client to the situation.

She kept on saying things such as, 'I can't trust'... 'I was annoyed by her'... 'I don't know if I can work with her because...' and so on. So I asked my client, who or what she meant by the 'I' when she spoke about herself. She came straight out with it: 'I guess my ego', was her reply.

I absolutely knew what I had to do next. She had been a manager for about three years; she had completed a management and leadership qualification. She was becoming very skilled at First Level Leadership (i.e. transactional leadership); reasonable at Second Level (transformational) and was starting to push into Third Level understanding. So I knew that she was ready for this exercise.

I asked her if she would like to do a mindfulness exercise. She seemed very enthused by the possibility. 'OK, I'd like you to sit back comfortably in your chair and look at the sign on the wall opposite.' 'Look at the sign for a few moments, then tell me, does it take any effort to see the sign?' 'No', came the answer. 'Do you have to think hard to see the sign or can you see it without much or any thought'. 'It takes no thought', came the answer.

'Is there any time delay in your seeing the sign and your being aware of it?', I asked. 'No time delay', came the answer. 'OK, so would it be true to say that seeing is thoughtless, effortless and timeless then?', I asked. 'Yes, that is correct', she said.

'OK, so now I would like you to really relax into being that which is seeing', I continued. She did so. 'Now, tell me, who or what is doing the seeing?', I asked. 'I am', she said. 'Great! So tell me, who or what is aware of the 'I' that you talk about?'

She thought for a bit, then said, 'my awareness'. 'Beautiful', I said. 'And this awareness, can you see it? Has it any shape or size?' 'No.' 'Has it any colour?' 'No'. 'Has it any beginning or any end?' 'No. It's just kind of emptiness', came her answer.

We continued like this ranging over other senses, such as hearing and sensations in the body. The same answer came back each time, that her highest self that was aware of all else, even the thing that she called, 'I', was no-thing, i.e. that it had no form and could not be seen. It was merely witnessing everything else.

Whilst in the state of experiencing this thing she called 'pure awareness', I continued. 'Is there anything here which should not be here…right in this very moment?' 'No'. 'Is there anything not here which should be here…right in this very moment?' 'No'. 'Can you find anything called 'the ego''? She laughed, 'no!'. 'Is there anything here called 'anger'?' 'No.' And so we continued. She had found a perfect place of nothingness. She had for the first time in her life, found herself. Her true identity as the ultimate witness, the ultimate place of no-thing consciousness.

This exercise is based upon a practice that we do in Awakening Coaching known as 'Radical Awakening'. It is a way of consciously guiding somebody into spaciousness, into the highest form of being. You can find out more about the Radical Awakening practice on my website at https://www.awakeningcoaching.co.uk.

Everybody has to go in and out of spaciousness every day in order to avoid going insane. But we're not aware of doing it. As in when you slip into sleep, especially dreamless sleep – you're slipping into unconscious spaciousness. This is effectively a state of 'no mind'. If people didn't have dreamless sleep, they'd go crazy! Radical Awakening brings you into conscious recognition of this spaciousness; the silent witness that cannot itself be seen. When we act from the knowledge of this place, of our true self, we expand our horizons as we recognise the reality that there are no limits, no boundaries to the truth of self.

When my client came out of her almost trance-like state, we revisited the problem that she had with her soon-to-be boss, and she recognised that the problem appeared to have dissolved. She could remember the problem, but the resonance had faded. She actually laughed at it. I then went on to ask her, 'deep within – the real you – is it a 'thing''? 'No, not really', she said.

'It's not something that I can touch'. Indeed - you can't see it or hear it or feel it. It's simply consciousness.

'So if you are not a thing, you are no-thing, or nothing. I too, am nothing. So what separates you and me? What separates nothing from nothing?', I asked. 'Nothing', she said.

Brilliant! Pure non-dual awareness. Oneness. I could see that she was visibly moved and awestruck by what she had just experienced and for the first time in her life, she was aware of who or what she really was. By transcending the illusion of self as a separate entity and by pulling away from being fully identified with her own narrative, my client had shifted into clear seeing of the truth.

This is of fundamental importance, because we cannot fully operate in the real world of people and problems as a leader if we are unable to see the reality of who or what we actually are. For this client, prior to this awakening experience into her true nature, she was living life through her ego. Conflict wasn't just possible, it was indeed absolutely unavoidable. Eckhart Tolle puts this process of awakening beautifully in 'The Power of Now':

> "The word *enlightenment* conjures up the idea of some superhuman accomplishment, and the ego likes to keep it that way, but it is simply your natural state of felt oneness with Being. It is a state of connectedness with something immeasurable and indestructible, something that, almost paradoxically, is essentially you and yet is much greater than you. It is finding your true nature beyond name and form. The inability to

> feel this connectedness gives rise to the illusion of separation, from yourself and from the world around you. You then perceive yourself, consciously or unconsciously, as an isolated fragment. Fear arises, and conflict within and without becomes the norm."

Thus 'transcendence', which means to be or to go beyond the range or limits (of your normal activity); or to surpass those previous limits, can only be achieved when you as a leader fully understand your true nature as an awakened being living out your highest purpose here on planet earth. It is the combination of truly knowing your highest self, the unbounded being of pure awareness, as well as the realisation of your purpose at this current time.

This absolute knowledge is of such importance to your transcendence as a leader that it forms the first foundational dimension of Transcendent Leadership. It shifts us into a completely different order of understanding, one in which we not only encompass the divine in our leadership practice, but in which we are able to fully experience the divinity of being. God is one with us in our truest essence.

If we come to this realisation from a place of ego, that is narcissism of the highest order. But if the divine spark within us realises that it is divine, i.e. the radiance within you realises that you yourself are the radiance - then you shift beyond the egoic realm into an altogether different place.

> "The eye with which I see God is the same eye with which God sees me."
>
> Meister Eckhart

Thus when you revolutionise your leadership practice to encompass the higher realms, the highest form of the 'self', then you allow the emergent self to grow up by revealing new, previously hidden knowledge in your practice. At the same time, you simultaneously wake up from the dream of being a separate and isolated individual. This is why the transcendence into Level Three is so vastly different to the shift in understanding and practice that takes place when moving from Level One to Level Two.

The time is long overdue for a whole new movement to take place across the planet to combine the leading edge of both the social science of leadership and the deepest and most abiding ancient wisdom and modern movements of spirit. This first dimension is the key to bringing these two aspects together into synchrony.

We are eternal spiritual beings having a short experience of life on earth in human form. Our mission, then, is to use the gifts that each of us has in a unique combination to learn, to love and to give. Pablo Picasso described this perfectly when he said, "The meaning of life is to find your gift. The purpose of life is to give it away." Brilliant.

If we have been blessed with leadership responsibility in any capacity, therefore, understanding of the dimensions of transcendence will enable us to realise those gifts to the fullest extent possible because we are no longer dependent only upon our own efforts and power, but we are now open to the abundant flow of the universe.

Thus 'awakening' to our true nature essentially forms the philosophical underpinning of Third Level, Transcendent Leadership. Without the transcendent radiance that the awakening can endow our leadership practice, we wallow in the shadows of a life spent as yet another stone cold bureaucrat or departmental middle manager.

I see so many people in the latter role, staggering through life like the un-dead of a Hollywood movie. The search for the revelation of everything is, for many people a fruitless one as they are either inert to the understanding that there is something they should even be searching for, or they simply don't know where to look.

A good analogy for thinking about this in relation to transcendence is by starting with Maslow's Hierarchy of human needs. We begin at the bottom of the hierarchy with the need to work to feed and clothe ourselves and to house ourselves and our families – basic survival needs in other words. We eventually emerge at the top of the hierarchy into a world of self-actualisation where we find meaning and purpose in what we do.

When you start the journey of transcendence, you will be clearing the heart of self-based ambition, of ego. You will find it so much easier to forgive, to heal, to love. You will be incorporating aspects of the divine in your understanding and your daily practice. As such, the top of the hierarchy is no longer personal self-actualisation that begins and ends with the small egoic self. Rather, as your understanding develops, you burst through the top of the hierarchy into a more profound dimension; you transcend the limited humanness of the hierarchy and become one with something beyond the self. Thus I would argue that there is a higher stage than self-actualisation. When we move to the next level of development, beyond traditional understanding, we encounter a new and emerging level I call 'self-transcendence'.

As we cleanse the heart of this sense of self, of personal ambition, we begin to live from the heart, from the centre of our being. We experience unfoldment from within. Ambition shifts from being directed inwards at ourselves to being directed outwards into the world. We shift from getting to giving. The boundaries that separate the inner world from the outer world begin to dissipate and in so doing, the schism that creates contraction and stress so too, dissipates. When there is no inner and no outer, the great divide that creates conflict and anxiety is transcended.

This level is admittedly, rather radical and thus outside normal, reductive understanding. This is because when you transcend your own humanity, you open up to being in your full potential in terms of realising your purpose on this planet. In transcending yourself, the 'small' you dissolves and you open new lines of connection to the Universe itself. It is no longer about you, your ambition, your needs. Paradoxically, the ultimate fulfilment of 'self' needs can only come about when you move *beyond* the self.

When the self is present, the self becomes the trap, the net that constrains the ultimate development of that same self. Healing of the delusion of self therefore needs to happen before self-mastery can occur, because in order to master the 'self', you have to give up the illusion of the self being at the centre of everything. Otherwise, you will always come from a place of limited energy, a place of pushing, a place of self-effort.

You transcend this level of self by waking up and growing up: waking up to the knowledge of who or what you truly are (revelation), both in terms of your true nature and in terms of your purpose as an eternal spirit walking the planet in human form; then growing up to recognise the leverage you have - the tools and the power at your disposal - subtle energies, states of awareness and states of realisation. Finally, a full understanding of your motivations, that is to say, waking up to the brilliance and the genius that are your unique gifts to give away.

Combine revelation, motivation and leverage and you have the ingredients for a transcendent revolution. It is at this moment that we hit the tipping point that shakes us clear of any last vestige of career-based drudgery. When we step through into transcendence, we come into our full potential; we lean into presence and spirit begins to pour through us with compassion, with creativity, with connection that radiates love and energy to those around us.

The first half of my career, a time spanning a full two decades, was spent in the realm of self-centred ambition. I knew that I had to accumulate knowledge and experience and certificates; things to populate the CV. I had to try ever harder. I had to compete. I had to win. I had to be seen to strive. I had to be *seen* to win. Eventually the sheer effort, based in my own humanity, nearly killed me. I had been managing nearly two thousand staff for around four years, and I was being interviewed for the next level of management. I was driven by fear of failure, was somewhat burnt out, and I was desperate to consolidate upon what I had achieved. And this was the point at which I was broken. At a subsequent interview I didn't give of my best; I was quiet, my sparkle had gone. It was the best thing that could have happened to me in retrospect, because it prevented me from blindly stumbling on further in my own human power.

I didn't get the job. Neither did they reject me. The interview panel knew that I had more to offer; they knew that something was wrong, and I was offered the opportunity for a further interview, an opportunity that I turned down. At the time, I was working on instinct; it just did not fill me with happiness to continue in the process. In retrospect, I know that there was a power higher than me gently guiding me to a job that would allow me to flourish within myself. I returned to a job that I loved; I loved the people, I loved returning to a position of community and systems leadership; I returned to a place where healing could happen which led to me resuming my journey towards self-mastery and finally the breakthrough of transcendence itself.

Once I had emerged into this new dimension of transcendence, I operated almost unconsciously in this domain for well over a year. It was a year of seemingly miraculous realisations, of synchronicities, of growth, of love, of quite extraordinary achievements. Gradually, the recognition that I had broken through into a whole new dimension of leadership, dawned upon me. It was from this place that I came to see the level of self-transcendence that existed beyond Maslow's Hierarchy. I was becoming ever more conscious of what was emerging, and then sought to make sense of it and codify it through reflection and contemplation. The code came together to form the eight dimensions of Transcendent Leadership.

I speak many times in these foundational chapters of paradox being at the heart of all truth. I recognised around this time that I was surrounded by paradox. My nursing and therapy teams seemed happier than anywhere else in the county, despite the fact that they were doing more work and seeing more patients than anywhere else. On paper, they should have been drained and burnt-out, but this simply was not apparent. Turnover and sickness were the lowest anywhere. Team members were recognised by awards at national level. Our team prevented more unnecessary acute hospital admissions than anywhere else in the country (measured by an England-wide indicator called the 'Standardised Admission Ratio'). We discharged patients back home faster than anywhere else; we had fewer delayed transfers of care than anywhere else in the county and fewer emergency readmissions. At the time of writing, comparator teams in the county have 45, 32, 29 and 27 patients medically fit and awaiting discharge back home. My team has just two, and one of them is wrongly coded, so it should be only one!

At the same time, my team has the most elderly population of patients, which should result in a longer length of stay due to their complexity and frailty; it should also be more problematic to discharge them. In fact, we are not merely performing a little better than everywhere else; we are actually on a different level altogether. We are happier, have less stress, more energy….the harder we work, the more time we seem to have, and personally, the more and more I love my team and love my job.

It just felt that nobody in my team was any longer coming from a place of ego. Whilst we were performing well, there was no sense of competition. Leaders in my team simply seemed to enjoy what was happening all around them. The notion that the small, egoic self is fully in control and fully capable was increasingly notable by its absence. The team had arrived into a place of wholeness, a place of sovereignty, of balance, of harmony, of knowledge.

The journey towards transcendence therefore has to necessarily involve your passing through the calm waters of healing; it is as much about your throwing off the shackles of self-ambition and careerism as anything. This burden needs releasing from you in order for the deep, transformative healing powers of the universe to release you, to let you experience a metamorphosis into the leader that you were always meant to be. It is as if you are becoming as naked as a baby all over again; a rebirth into the 'you' that has been hiding beneath the hogwash of this earthly career person ever since you left college. The rebirthed 'you' will become the most radiant version of you there has ever been. Your very radiance will be one of the most transformative acts you can ever experience as a leader. There will be little or no human effort on your part; the radiant energy of just being will become an infectious act in and of itself.

I talk above about releasing burden. This is central to the notion of healing and of transcending. Let me explain by using an extreme example. Could there be any greater release of burden than death? Could there be any greater release at all? In his moving and profound song, Lazarus, recorded shortly before his death, David Bowie sings,

> "I've got nothing left to lose
> I'm so high it makes my brain whirl
> Dropped my cell phone down below"

He is saying that he is released. Released even from his cell phone, from any further striving; released from the human form. The Radical Awakening practice I described earlier in the chapter indeed gives us an insight into the death of self. It is spiritual awakening. When we engage with this practice, we transcend the ego, we transcend the small self, the self of mind, of thoughts, of body, of our past, of our hopes and aspirations; indeed, the stuff of self that Bowie describes as being on the cell phone – our Facebook profile and so on. All of this dissipates and we are left with only our true nature as divine being. There is only the no-thing of self that remains. We transcend the world of form. We are healed from that limited identity, the identity on the curriculum vitae.

It is important to note, however, that when we transcend the self, that self hasn't actually gone anywhere. You can have an awakening experience in which you will know the true nature of your being. However, at the same time, you will still be living in the real world. My friend, Reverend Paul John Roach, often quotes Jack Kornfield, 'After the Ecstasy, the Laundry!'. This stage of opening to your own awakening can be challenging and painful at times. It may take months or years to fully reconcile these two polarities of your own being – the human and the divine. To go from a peak experience and transition within minutes into a nitty-gritty problem, or to have to deal with people stuck in their ego can at first be a wrench.

There is a way to bring peak experience and reality into coherence, however. The key to healing, to reconciling the polarity is in learning how to embody spirit. How to be fully in the ego-transcendent stage of development whilst at the same time living in a world where ego abounds. Once we have experientially learnt how to reconcile the two, we come to an abiding sense of rest and wellbeing. Then from that place of serenity, the universe births creativity and inspiration.

When we figure out our place as an eternal spiritual being that is able to operate freely without encumbrance in the world of form and of ego, we experience a great liberation. Living in but transcending this world at Third Level opens us up to the great radiance of being. You will have a rock solid sense of self, of purpose and mission and destiny. When you ascend to the top of the mountain, beyond Maslow's hierarchy, you will open to what Ken Wilber calls the 'Indigo Stage of Consciousness', which has been summarised by Barrett Brown as:

> Main focus: Being, non-controlling consciousness; witnessing flux of experience and states of mind. Qualities: Emergence of a perspective that is ego-transcendent or universal; people holding this stage of consciousness seem to "...experience themselves and others as part of ongoing humanity, embedded in the creative ground, fulfilling the destiny of evolution" (Cook-Greuter, 2002, p. 32); consciousness ceases to appear as a constraint but rather as one more phenomenon that can be foreground or background; an integration of feelings of belongingness and separateness occurs; multiple points of view can be taken effortlessly; the pattern of constant flux

and change becomes the context for feeling at home; one is able to respect the essence in others, no matter how different they may be; one is in tune with their life's work as "a simultaneous expression of their unique selves" and as part of their shared humanity."

Barrett C. Brown, Integral Institute April 3, 2006

Compare this with Barrett Brown's description of the ego, or red stage of consciousness, from the same paper:

"Main focus: Own immediate needs, opportunities, self-protection
Description: First step toward self-control of impulses; sense of vulnerability and guardedness; fight/flight response is very strong; very attack-oriented and win/lose in nature; short-term horizon; focus on concrete things and personal advantage; sees rules as loss of freedom; feedback heard as an attack
How influences others: Takes matter into own hands, coerces, wins fight."

Can you see the immense void between the two states of developmental consciousness? As a Transcendent Leader, you will make the shift from the egoic stage to divine being. To begin with, this will be something that you are conscious of, that fills your thoughts. The longer you live from this place, however, the egoic sense of self that you have been looking back on will begin to fade. Your true identity will become more and more unified and peaceful.

At this point, dealing with the many people that you will continue to encounter at the egoic level of consciousness will become less and less of a struggle. Think of how Jesus used to actively seek out the dispossessed, the sinful, the abusers of power. And think of how he dealt with them. There was no struggle, there was no inner battle for Jesus. He came from a place of truth, of equanimity and of peace, so fully identified was he with his divinity. At this stage, consciousness stops turning back on itself and looking at where it has come from. All is unified. From this point, the journey as a Transcendent Leader is one of connection with everything, it is a great unifying process; whereby heaven and earth come together as one. You will fully embody your spirituality, your divine radiance and your mission. It is a liberation of the highest order.

This leads us to being able to state the first dimension of Transcendent Leadership: Knowledge of your true nature is a necessary pre-condition and the key to becoming a Transcendent Leader.

Summary of Practices and Reflections in this dimension:

- Radical Awakening   30

Chapter 2

The Second Dimension: Seeing

Revealing Your Mission

In Second Level leadership practice, people often talk about 'stretch targets'. Think into this phrase a little. How does it sound to you? Now move from your head to your heart and feel into it. How does it make you feel? How does it resonate with you? If your boss came to you and said, 'right, we're going to set you up with some stretch targets', how would you react? 'Fabulous!, I absolutely love being set stretch targets!'. If you're anything like me, that's really not how I tend to react. Rather than being something expansive that makes me feel excited and invigorated, it makes me feel like I am contracting. It feels as if it's something that somebody else is doing *to me* rather than *with me*.

Now consider how I phrase the same kind of thing in my coaching practice. I normally use a two-phase question. Firstly, I ask people, 'what is your greatest longing?'. This is a fabulous question first proposed to me by my teacher, Arjuna Ardagh. The word that I associate with this is 'expansive'. It puts me back into the frame of mind when I was in my late teens/early twenties, when I naturally felt such licence to dream. It's the time before choices have been made and paths established; the time when nothing has yet been closed down.

My personal answer to this question, apart from the most important ones of love, family and living a life aligned with the divine, is around being the best version of myself possible. I believe that I am an eternal spiritual being who is having a short sojourn here on planet earth in human form. As such, I'm here to learn, to love and to give the best of myself.

The second question is equally marvellous and magical. Here it is: 'What is your longest reach?' In and of itself, this question has transformed my life in the last few years. It carries with it immense charge. It is one of the most powerful questions that anyone can ever ask themselves. It really threw me when I first heard it. In fact it rather stunned me. Then I took it to be a challenge. Shortly afterwards through further contemplation, it felt more like an invitation. Later still, it began to feel like a gift. This question led directly to my wife and I buying land in Paraguay and then setting about reforesting it. This then led to us setting up a funding campaign to protect the Atlantic Rainforest.

To some these things might sound rather insignificant. There's always somebody that has done greater things than you. But if you'd told me ten or twenty years ago that this was within my reach, I'd have been stunned by it. I still am to be honest. But without these two questions, these things would never have happened.

So when you set targets in Third Level Leadership, these powerful questions are a fabulous place to start. It is another example of the almost supernatural charge that is contained when you transcend from Second Level.

Why not challenge yourself right now by asking yourself these same two questions:

1) What is your greatest longing?

2) What is your longest reach?

Look for up to ten answers to each. Most people do around five to eight but just write what is meaningful to you.

Once you have done this, you might like to consider how this aligns with your current or future planned leadership role.

When answering the questions, I invite you to be very aware of a key ingredient that is absolutely inherent in these two questions. I'm talking about 'passion'. Is it even possible to answer these questions without passion? This is your *greatest* reach, don't forget. GREATEST! That cannot possibly come attached without passion. As Georg Wilhelm Friedrich Hegel said, "Nothing great in the world was accomplished without passion."

I would go so far as to say that it is impossible to operate at Third Level if there's a lack of passion. Big picture and mission are prerequisites for passion. See the bigger picture, see your true mission in that, and passion will flow. If it doesn't, or won't, then you either have serious blockages that need resolving, or you're not going big enough.

Passion is ordinarily defined as a strong and barely controlled emotion. Applied to the field of romance, this is really quite apt. However, in the world of organisations, the emotional element might be something that on a day to day basis, we're able to rather more easily keep in check. Nonetheless, without passion, it's difficult to have a vision. Without passion, others will not be drawn to follow you. Without passion, there is no heartfelt meaning. Without passion, there is no excitement or enthusiasm. Without passion, you will find stress and burnout and pointless meandering and clock-watching.

Passion lies at the heart of the Third Level leader. How much passion do you see at First Level, at transactional level? None probably, because the mechanistic elements at this level can be performed completely devoid of passion. You can shift elements of First Level over to a computer and they are just as effective. The beauty of Third Level leadership is that no computer in the world can get anywhere near it because it comes from the heart, the higher self, through esoteric practice, through creativity, through source and through the channelling of spirit.

So turn back to the powerful questions above. When you answered them for yourself, how did you feel? Connect with the frequency in your heart and let that frequency radiate out from you with your team and within your organisation. This is one of the keys to transmission for the Transcendent Leader. Show your passion, do not hold back, and the vibration of your passion will radiate into every corner of your organisation and beyond. Jesus attested to this:

"Neither do men light a candle, and put it under a bushel, but on a candlestick; and it giveth light unto all that are in the house. Let your light so shine before men, that they may see your good works, and glorify your Father which is in heaven."

King James Bible, 1611, Matthew, 5:15 and 5:16.

Steve Jobs was the Chairman, Chief Executive Officer, and co-founder of Apple Inc. As a leader, he was a disrupter of existing paradigms. He once said, "I want to put a ding in the universe". Remember what we said about 'your furthest reach?!" Well, putting a ding in the universe really has to be up there! He also once wonderfully said, "You have to be burning with an idea, or a problem, or a wrong that you want to right. If you're not passionate enough from the start, you'll never stick it out." This is so crucial to the Transcendent Leader. I know of no great leader who wasn't burning with passion for the mission that they had set out upon.

Try this as a practice: Feel into the things that get you passionate like Steve Jobs. What is burning inside of you? Write down a list of these things. They are the things that you can refer to when the going gets tough, rather like a sign post. I call these your 'True North Markers', as if they are written onto a sign, directing you back to where your attention needs to be.

Examples of my own True North Markers are:
- Meaningful connection and spending time with family.
- Giving my gifts away to other people.
- Being creative – always letting spirit channel through me on a project.
- Spending time in meditation.
- Always doing something positive for the ecosystem.

You might also write a list of questions that can bring you back into alignment when your attention gets diverted. These are your 'Compass Questions'. For me, the list looks something like this:
- Is my heart singing in this moment?
- Am I feeling rested?
- What is most important to me?
- What am I going to serve?
- Am I feeling energised?
- Am I burning with passion for my mission?

- Am I distracted with things that don't actually matter?
- What am I going to orientate my life around?
- What do I really value most?
- Do I feel like the best version of me…right now?
- Do the people around me feel like I am giving them attention…right now?

Try writing down your own list of True North Markers and Compass Questions. Keep them to hand, maybe copy them into your notes section on your smartphone.

Having your True North Markers and Compass Questions to hand is so important. It's a great first step to maintain the correct state of consciousness for when the going gets hard. It will. It always will. This is life; it's a rocky road of learning. That's what happens. The secret is not to ensure that it never gets rocky; the secret is to know how to respond and how to maintain conscious focus on the direction that you set at a time when the road was smooth and when you had clarity of vision.

When your passion first began to materialise, you may have felt an energy searing through you as if you had first fallen in love. This is the feeling, the state of consciousness that you have to return to time and time again in order to attain alignment and to manifest the goal. That is because when you find yourself being buffeted by a storm in your path of realising that passion, your original state of consciousness needs to be brought back to the fore. You have to deal with the rocky path from that state of consciousness, not from a state of consciousness of the ego or from the conditioned mind or the worried mind or a mind overcome by cortisol or fight/flight/freeze mode.

Overcoming obstacles from this level, the transactional level, simply will not work.

Steve Jobs had to overcome all manner of obstacles in being able to realise his vision for computing and connection. The only way in which he was able to do this was at every stage to maintain his focus on the original dream. Thus he met every attack from the standpoint of the transcendent mind. He wasn't merely transacting (First Level); he wasn't even transforming (Second Level). In order to be as disruptive and radical as he was, only Third Level, the transcendent (remember, this means, 'beyond or above the range of normal or physical human experience') would do. If the roadblocks to your transcendent vision come from the First Level, then simply by using First Level techniques, you will not overcome them. If your vision was crafted from Third Level consciousness then your response to any turmoil along the way has to also be crafted from Third Level consciousness.

Again, if you struggle to maintain the right response to difficulty, turn to your absolute truth, as defined by your compass questions. Ask yourself the question, 'who or what am I going to serve in this moment?'. Look at the problems presenting themselves to you and ask yourself if they are absolute or relative problems? In other words, how deep do they go? Do they challenge your True North Markers or are they merely artefacts of day to day life?

If you are still getting stuck trying to prise yourself away from the transactional world, then go bigger. Remind yourself that you are an eternal spiritual being having a short experience in human form, in order to learn, to love and to grow. Then return to your compass questions. Go really deep. Look into the very nature of your being. What are you doing here on this planet at this time? When you succeed at delivering your passion, your mission, and you look back at your life when you're on your death bed, will you have succeeded in your walk? Will you have managed to put some kind of a ding in the fabric of the universe? Will you even be able to remember the multitude of daily concerns and obstacles you faced in your trajectory from dream to manifestation? Who or what did you really serve when the going got tough? Did you serve the world, the naysayers, small minded people and critics, or did you serve the higher self, the higher vision, your higher truth?

When you dive deeply into your divinity and open to God, you will experience an inner unity. Essentially, your compass stops flying around all over the place and it will indeed settle on your True North. This doesn't mean that you don't get new ideas; it doesn't mean that new opportunities won't arise. These all reside on the tactical plane. True North resides on the strategic plane. It's the really big picture. Values if they are values at all do not shift. When I did this work a few years ago, it so firmly cemented my place on the planet. Mind-based narratives of doubt and the noise in my internal operating system dissolved until I was left with Absolute Certainty about who I was, what I was doing here and what was really, genuinely important.

I write Absolute Certainty as a proper noun not only to emphasise its importance, but also to reference it as one of the principles, the cornerstones of my coaching practice. **The greatest gift I can give my clients is the Absolute Certainty that they already have everything that they need to have - they are already who they need** to be. If I find that a client isn't dropping deeply enough in, it's because I myself am not dropping deeply enough in. But when I have Absolute Certainty, then the client will also have that Absolute Certainty, too.

This may sound rather trite to some, but the simple truth is that I now have no doubt over my own place in this world as a spiritual being and my purpose whilst here in human form. Indeed, my wife recently was listening to a Christian podcast about doubt and faith, and she turned to me and asked me, 'what are your doubts?'. Since I made the shift into a non-dual understanding of the universe and divinity, the honest truth is that I have no doubt. I now have only knowledge. This can sit very uncomfortably with some Christian teaching whereby adherents are trapped in an endless cycle of doubt-faith; the latter necessary because of the dualistic separation of understanding that will always produce an abundance of doubt. It's like a metaphysical labyrinth of endless circularity. Doubt and faith are continuums on a plane of polarity. One cannot exist without the other.

I see so many people trapped in this prison of duality, but until you reach the point of singularity, of non-duality where you can rest in Absolute Certainty, you will never find true peace. Now when I hit periods of turmoil, instead of being thrown around like a boat in a storm, I observe, I act, but I don't identify with the turmoil. Once you can deal with uncertainty and turmoil from your deepest 'self', the place that never changes, it can feel as you are connected to an immovable rock. You are firmly anchored in place because the origin of your knowledge and understanding is itself immovable, i.e. the divinity of all that is.

I recall once having a supervision session with one of my senior managers, David, when I worked in a mental health organisation. He was embarked upon a test of change which was fundamental and huge in its scope. David had until recently been a technical subject matter expert. His experience of general management was at the time about one year old. The change programme he was leading was designed by him and his team to meet a challenge that I had laid down for him. Nothing of its kind had ever been attempted in our county before. Two weeks in, it was working very well, with the exception of a vocal core of staff who were threatening to go to the unions. Their cosy work-lives had been disturbed. The new system had exposed the fact that they had been working at around one-third capacity for years. They were determined to make life tough for David.

Now David had come a very long way in a short space of time. I knew that he was ready for this. He knew in his core who he was and what his mission consisted of. I could tell that he was feeling the strain. So I coached him through this from the point of view of Absolute Certainty. He instantly hooked into this. Indeed, he himself told me that he knew that he would maintain his focus at Third Level. If people wanted to drag him down into the mire of falsehood, victimhood and confrontation, they could try all they liked, but they would never dislodge him from doing the right thing from an awakened consciousness.

We can therefore see the importance of getting our consciousness right; immersing ourselves in our True North values and aims, and maintaining the correct state of being. When we truly know what or who we serve in our walk here on earth, nothing can divert us from truth, because truth is absolute and all gossip, resistance, office politics and the bleating of interest groups is relative.

Once you're hooked into the steadfastness of truth, your job is elevated from not being merely a job to being a divine mission. This is one of the central principles of Transcendent Leadership, that it is utterly impossible to achieve Third level if you are treating the subject of the leadership (your job, your sports team etc.) as if it were a task or a chore.

The spark of magic can only be lit if you are connected to the subject of your leadership on a much more fundamental level of truth. You have to be living your mission. This means ensuring that you have Absolute Certainty in terms of what that mission is. I will speak extensively about the notion of surrender later in the book, and it is a theme that runs throughout Transcendent Leadership. I strongly suspect that each of us has a mission or various missions that are pre-destined for us. It is the thing that is 'ours to do'. It's the thing that we are perfectly designed to do. And when we connect with it, it is then that the energy of the universe flows through us.

Some people live an entire lifetime with no idea of what this mission is, what their greatest gifts are and therefore how to outwork that mission in their brief time here on the earth. You may even be floundering, unsure exactly what this thing is that might well be waiting for you. It may be calling you right now and you're just not listening.

It is often the case that we are blind and deaf to the thing that has been trying to reach out to us, the thing that is right under our nose already. The more we become attuned to spotting these moments, these chances, the more confirmation we have that we are on the right path.

In my coaching practice, I help people connect with their deepest self, their ultimate longing, their highest purpose. It's invariably the case that the people that are most fulfilled in their life seem to not be those people that are constantly turned in on themselves, who spend every waking hour in meditation and contemplation. Quite the contrary - the people who are most fulfilled are those people who understand the bigger picture, who understand what they are doing with their life. They open themselves up to something bigger than themselves and they become a channel for the flow of the universe. The creativity that manifests through people when they take this step is phenomenal. Such people are absolutely on fire, they begin to shine like the sun. Amazing things happen!

The incredible thing as well is that when we surrender to this bigger force, we don't really know exactly what's going to begin to flow through our lives. It's like an incredible roller-coaster. In my experience, when we decide with our head and from a position of greed or lower intentions what it is that we want to manifest, it doesn't always pan out. But when we recognise our gifts and ask the divine to take what is ours and use it in a spirit of excitement and infinite possibility, then incredible things begin to happen.

So let me share with you an opportunity that has come to me through this life-force, the flow of the universe. I honestly could never have made this up. I wouldn't ever have even thought of it, however hard I had tried.

Here's just a snippet of the string of things that have happened:

I get a place to read Economics at Claire College, Cambridge. My geography teachers fail to teach a single subject that comes up on one of my Geography A Level papers. I get a 'B'. I needed an 'A'. I go to Southampton University instead. There I become friends with a Major in the Salvation Army. Through one of his friends, I meet somebody who works in a Salvation Army home in Paraguay (o, yes, another string of coincidences leads me to live for a year in a dance academy in Paraguay....long story!). Through these connections, I meet three charming triplet sisters, including Isabel, who later came to England and married me!

One of Isabel's sisters marries an awesome man - an ecologist and land manager for a Catholic retreat. He manages hundreds of hectares of organic farmland and forest in the beautiful Cordillera region of Western Paraguay. He is an expert in reforestation and has himself planted tens of thousands of trees in the Cordillera. He and my sister-in-law help facilitate our purchasing of two acres of organic land and we start reforesting a slice of Atlantic Rainforest that we now own.

.....all of which brings us to the present day. Isabel and I realised just how easy and relatively cheap it is to protect existing ancient rainforest, as well as to reforest - to re-grow what has already been lost.

So we decided that we wanted to share this opportunity with other people. People sponsor donkeys; rather more importantly in my view, they sponsor children in

Africa. So why not sponsor a tree, we thought! Why not sponsor some square metres of a rainforest? So we set up a fund for doing precisely that. What is more, when people hire me as an Awakening Coach, rather than take a fee personally, I ask clients to contribute towards the reforestation programme. It thus creates a beautiful circle of giving and of growth – I love coaching, the client meets their objectives; a rainforest gets replenished!

OK, so you might critique this by saying that everything that happens in our lives is ultimately the result of a string of unlikely events. True, but in Awakening Coaching, I have learnt to be aware, to be awakened to those meaningful coincidences. The ones that just seem to have something more to them. The extraordinary coincidences that seem to carry a charge, that seem to be beckoning me on, almost daring me to push on a door, to take a peek under a particular stone. And this one for me was screaming at me, there was nothing subtle about it!

I found myself in a position whereby I could simply and relatively easily buy rainforest and plant trees. And I could do it on behalf of people who would love to do it but who don't have the knowledge and contacts that I have. How could I NOT respond to that one?! It almost felt like a door I would have to resist being flung open rather than having to push it open myself. So I didn't resist. I let the door open. I let the Universe sing.

We can all do this, whatever the nature of our calling is. Open your heart and listen to what the Universe is nudging you to do. For there is surely a path of 'coincidences' in your life that is just waiting for you to recognise them as not actually coincidences but rather an invitation to manifest brilliance! Be very suspicious of seeming coincidences. If you find that they carry a charge, get you excited, then treat them not as coincidences but as something much more profound. They are so often an invitation by a power bigger than you to push open the door and to fulfil your walk on this beautiful planet of ours. Everybody can let the Universe sing!

Alongside this, there is a more structured way in which you can explore the areas in which you should be operating. I believe that you are perfectly designed to be the leader in the area in which your qualities shine. But how to discover what those qualities are? There's an exercise that I use as an Awakening Coach which will reveal this. For a full explanation, take a look at Chapter 20 of my book, 'Mind-Spirit Detox', "Know Your Genius". Here's an extract from the practice:

> Think of 10 to 14 people who have known you for at least a couple of years. Preferably choose people who you've known since you were young.
> You need to pick people who you do not work with, but preferably not close family. We need to find people who know you as you, i.e. not the job role you do. For example, you might be a great lawyer, but that might not be the real you – you might be doing something as a career that you felt obliged to do, rather than the thing that plays out your highest qualities – the gift that you were meant to give back to the world.
>
> Send the people you have chosen an email, asking them to write down 12 qualities that they think that you have, keeping it to one word for each quality.
>
> Once you have your results, put the words into a spreadsheet (or do this manually on paper if you prefer). To begin with, just put the name of the person who responded, and enter the list of words they gave you under their name.

Then copy and paste all of the words and put them into a single column.
Sort the column from A to Z.
This should begin to put similar words together.
Do a bit of manual sorting/sifting. If you have similar words, e.g. 'energy', 'driven', then group them if they have the same fundamental meaning.
Where you have any quality that is just a single one, that only one person has written, then discard that quality in the sorting process.
Now list the qualities starting with the one that most people have mentioned – typically this might be a word which 6–8 people chose about you. You will then get a few with 3–6 respondents typically; then a number with a couple of respondents.
This is the sorted list of your top qualities!
These are the brilliances that you have to offer the world.
Put together, they form your genius.

Now comes the contemplative aspect. Take time out, maybe over a few days, and keep your sorted list close by; print it out or copy it into notes on your smartphone.
Gently and gradually contemplate these qualities. What do they mean? Are you in the right day job to offer your genius to the world? Is the day job not the main focus of your life – are you living out your genius in other ways – volunteering, caring, leading groups, creative projects etc.?

For some people, the word 'genius' seems a little overcooked for a list of positive qualities. But think about it – you haven't prompted the people you've asked in any way whatsoever. There are over 60,000 adjectives in the English language – the fact that you can group some common ones that your friends have chosen to describe your qualities indicates that these really must be qualities that you have to offer the world. And given the immense number of words that could apply to any individual, the chances that any other person on the planet has the same list as you have is vanishingly small.
This is a really big deal! You are an eternal spiritual being living a very short life in human form in order to experience, to love, to show compassion, and to learn and to grow. God made you with this unique combination of qualities. This

combination is therefore as individual to you as a fingerprint. So that has to mean something, right? This fingerprint therefore represents your genius in the world. If you find this difficult to accept, try looking again at the 'Golden Shadow' practice, and the words of scripture at the top of this practice.

Just consider this – how many times in a lifetime do you get a list of your own qualities in this way? Probably this is the first ever time (distinct from work-based 360-degree feedback exercises which mostly focus only on your ability at a particular job/task, and which are much more prone to 'projection' on the part of the observer).

So do not underestimate the importance of this. If you describe that combination of qualities as anything less than your genius, then you fail to understand the magnitude of this practice. Remember, though, that it's only really genius if you a) figure out what it all means when seen as a whole; and b) do something with it – put it into practice.

This is the universe talking to you. Do not disregard the outcome of this exercise. It will point you in the direction to which you need to be looking. Remember, only by out-working your mission will you be leading at the transcendent level. And your mission will inevitably be perfectly designed by the universe to be using your own, personal genius. Nobody else's – YOURS! Your own, unique genius and your mission are in perfect alignment. If you have not yet discovered what that is, then use these techniques to start searching. It's there for you. Right now.

Before I move on, I would like to shine a light on some peculiarities of this particular mode of operating. As I have already said, I work intensively with people for a few weeks at a time using the world's most incredible technique – that of coaching.

Coaching works brilliantly for people who simply want to become a better version of themselves, but they come to me because don't know how to or where to start. People are often stuck in their journey through life, not knowing which decision branch to follow; they may be confused, have too many options or indeed, their mind may be blocking off potential and brilliant options due to self doubt or limiting beliefs.

But there is one little corner of coaching can often be the one in which people make the most breakthroughs in their lives. It's the one that involves that strangest of things, namely 'polarities', especially when combined with paradox.

I had a social media debate with a fundamentalist recently. The debate continued day after day for about a week. Being an ex-fundamentalist myself, I could predict with near exact certainty what each of his next arguments would be. And it occurred to me that this gentleman was trapped in a two dimensional decision tree. It didn't appear to be making him happy, only rather confrontational.

You see, every decision he made had to be either one or the other; black or white, right or wrong. He was living in a world of forced duality, where the rules of the game meant winners and losers. And the winners were a very, VERY small section of the population that obviously included him and his kinsmen. Into the losers pile he threw all Catholics (1.2 billion of what he called, 'cultists'); all Anglicans (because they are attempting to reconcile with Catholics - another 84 million to add to the list); all liberal protestants, not to mention humanists, Buddhists, Muslims and so on and so on. Whilst engaging with this chap on this level, nothing was created. No good came from the conversation. The two dimensional decision tree leads only to dead-ends. But there was something in this man that I liked. I saw passion and certainty.

I invited him to my house with a mutual friend and we connected over our love of music and South America. As I write, he is in Mendoza in Argentina, using some of the Spanish I helped him with, whilst working on a community project. We continue to develop new ideas around poverty-relief projects on an ongoing basis.

Thus by opening up to the Universe, I hope and trust that a new dimension of generative relationship is emerging in our friendship. In this, I find paradoxical polarities. In this example, on the one hand, I had met a man who, on a human level, wound me up more than anybody has in recent months, with his residing at the opposite end of the spiritual polarity to me – him being a closed-minded fundamentalist, and me being an open-minded mystic. Despite this, I had a deep sense that there was a place within this relationship where spirit was trying to get in. In my experience, the most amazing answers and breakthroughs come when trying to reconcile polarities. This is the place where paradox exists. And truth resides in paradox. Not only truth, but limitless possibility and brilliance.

Paradox is defined as, 'a seemingly absurd or contradictory statement or proposition…'. In this case, by embracing the paradox of opening up in friendship to somebody that I had had something of an on-line row with, produced a generative relationship in which our divergent views came together to support a really positive community project.

Let me illustrate with an example from my own life. I am English and my wife Paraguayan. Where should we live? The fundamentalist might suggest that the answer is in one country or the other. They often see the world as an 'either/or' universe. However, when faced with complexity, I like to remind myself that it is in fact a 'both/and' universe.

So we solved the polarity by continuing to reside in England, but, as I explained above, we bought a couple of acres of beautiful Paraguayan land with some wildlife-rich rainforest in it. Not only do we now have a stake in South America, but we can provide a space for the extended family to live in, and we have also been replanting the rainforest with endangered native hardwoods and fruiting palm trees for the birds.

This answer emerged to my wife and I as we opened to this paradoxical, both/and universe. We surrendered logical thinking and the outmoded, dualistic approach and let the answer emerge and flow through our consciousness. Even if we had discerned such a perfect answer using our logical faculties, the manifestation of the answer would then have been another difficult challenge to face.

But the source of the answer lies in the universe residing within us, or more accurately, we are the universe and the universe is us. So by surrendering the answer to the universe, the universe also manifests the answer back into the world of form. If that sounds a bit abstract, let me illustrate it for you:

Old paradigm - dualistic thinking:

1) Work out using logical thought and struggle with what the best answer is; maybe you can list the possibilities and score/rank each one. Discover the answer.

2) Again, using logical thought, search using your own power for the way in which to fulfil the top ranking option, i.e. how to manifest the answer. In this case, if the answer is to buy a house in Paraguay then you need to search for it using a lot of hard work and on-line estate agents.

New paradigm - surrender to the universe, accept paradox and reconcile polarities:

1) Surrender and wait for the universe to reveal the perfect answer. Do it with a pure heart and clear intent. Release any mind-based, egoic consciousness. Let it go.

2) Once the answer emerges, surrender again in the knowledge that the perfect answer will manifest in the real world (the world of form).

When the answer emerges through surrender, you create heart-mind synchrony. You will feel a 'rightness' in your entire mind-heart-body system. A coherence will occur. There will be no contraction in the body as you ease into the emergent future.

This reconciliation of polarities that creates coherence is becoming more and more important in today's increasingly complex world. When we blindly polarise, we live a myopic world that pushes us away from other people. Learning to identify dualities and polarities and then understanding how to reconcile the contradictions and polarities is key to us becoming whole. When we remain fragmented and dualistic in our understanding, we create blockages to universal flow. When we strive for wholeness, we open the tap to the divine manifesting goodness in us and through us.

In our case, as we received knowledge that the answer was to buy land in Paraguay, we allowed the same universe that gave us the answer, to also manifest that answer. So instead of having to look really hard for the land, the land looked for us. At around the same time as we were allowing the answer to emerge, an elderly 'campesino' who needed to sell some land sought out my brother-in-law, and the rest is history. It was the perfect sized land in the perfect location at a very reasonable price.

The more sceptical of my friends and clients ask me what the mechanism is for this coherence to unfold. I have studied this area with a degree of obsessiveness and I think that the following is the best explanation available to us at this moment:

There is a field of information all around us; there are several similar theories about this. My two favourites are that of Dr Rupert Sheldrake who calls it the 'Morphic Field', and Dr Ervin Laszlo who calls it the 'Akashic Field'. I first came across this theory in a book recommended to me by my father, 'Grammatical Man: Information, Entropy, Language, and Life' by Jeremy Campbell. The theories are extensive and are essentially around the interplay of quantum physics and human biology. 'Let the field find you rather than the other way around' is the way to practise this in a nutshell - set out your intention and throw it out into the field. The answer, the *perfect* answer will come and find you out.

I have to admit that 'Grammatical Man' is very heavy going. But if you want a five minute short-cut to understanding how to let the field come to you, I'd recommend you look up 'The Legend of Bagger Vance Clip 2 Seeing the Field' on YouTube. This says it all! Understanding polarities, fields, paradox and manifestation is a wonderful thing. Maybe there's an answer to a problem that you have just waiting for you out there. Connect with the field. Be patient. Feel. Use Third Level understanding to gain knowledge.

We are now in a position to summarise the second dimension of Transcendent Leadership: Uncovering your greatest longing and longest reach within the field of consciousness will enable you to fully see your core mission in the world.

Summary of Practices and Reflections in this dimension:

- Greatest Longing   45

- Longest Reach   45

- True North Markers   48

- Compass Questions   48

- Who am I Going to Serve? 51

- Know Your Genius   58

- Reconcile Polarities   62

Chapter 3

The Third Dimension: Being

Becoming You

It's all about you. Is it? The truth lies in another paradox. It is both all about you and it is nothing about you. Both/and…all at once. Once you are able to read that sentence and understand and believe it - that you are both the everything and the nothing in leadership, then you will probably have got to near where you need to get to. Personal mastery of the eight dimensions is key to Transcendent Leadership, and this begins with truly becoming *you* by becoming one with your true nature.

I once led a team implementing a governance structure within a large London mental health organisation. One of the psychologists on my team told me about an exercise he did in his training around leadership and facilitation. He was part of a group sitting in a circle, of some dozen psychology graduates. One among them was the group leader. They were tasked with leading the group in an exercise. Everybody in the group would mark the group in how transparently and fluidly the exercise was led. And then and only then would the leader reveal themselves to the group. The task was to lead the group so well that the participants didn't even recognise who the leader was, so naturally did they have to do the leading.

In the same way, at times when your team is being led brilliantly at Third Level, it will almost seem as if you as a leader become translucent. The team will be flying once it has hit cruising altitude; you are watching, listening, monitoring, nudging. It's like hitting the perfect shot in tennis when you hit the ball from the sweet spot in the middle of the racket – it feels effortless, you hardly feel anything but the ball traces the perfect trajectory. Your very presence will be everything that the team needs; energy will be flowing through you; decisions will be taken in the right time by the right person at the right level. The energy flow becomes almost miraculous and this shifts as far away from the heroic leader model of leadership as you can possibly imagine. The notion of all of the energy coming from the human efforts of the 'great I am' at the front of the team becomes almost laughable in its anachronistic outworking. Hence the appearance of the nothingness, despite the parallel truth that it's also everything to do with your leadership.

This is totally at odds with the sense of nothingness that drives so many leaders in organisations today. Such leaders come from a negative place of lack, such as the need to prove a teacher or parent wrong when they told them that they'd amount to nothing. If leadership practice comes from a sense of lack, then it is impossible to practice 'nothingness' because of the presence of negative thought and resistance.

How then, do we banish thoughts of lack and of negativity from our minds? How do we detox the mind in order that we can practise transcendence? I spoke in chapter 3 about polarities. People often mistakenly think that the polarity of love is hate, when I would argue that the polarity of love is fear. Similarly, people think that the polarity of unhappiness is happiness. If you think about this for a minute, you'll see that this is nonsense. The polarity of happiness is actually lack of happiness, or more accurately, something which obscures your happiness. Think of it this way – what is the opposite of blue sky? It's not cloud. Cloud merely obscures or gets in the way of the blue sky. Blue sky is what we experience when there is an absence of cloud. In the same way, happiness is just there all the time; when we don't feel it, we merely feel the absence of unhappiness. Happiness is our natural being, our natural state.

When we live in the mind, we are not present to 'what is', because it becomes obscured by thoughts of the future or the past. By not being present to the 'now' moment, we unconsciously keep alive that which is obscuring our happiness. How much of our unhappiness is brought about by regretting the past or striving for a future state? Neither of these future or past states is in fact *real*. They can only be created in the mind, in the imagination. Conversely, when we practice being present, living in the only thing that is actually real, i.e. the eternal 'now', unhappiness cannot survive. The unhappiness becomes like clouds or mist being burnt off by the sun.

Thus we give our unhappiness life by giving it our time and our attention through the endless churning of thought that is unrelated to reality, i.e. the present moment. When we begin to recognise this, we realise that we have the power to kill off unhappiness by coming back to presence. When we return to presence, we surrender to what is real and through this surrender, spiritual energy begins to flow. When spiritual energy flows, we become free of polarities. The reality of presence is nothingness, i.e. 'presence' reveals 'what is' and 'what is' is nothingness. Sure, there are still 'things' – things we can observe, sense, feel and so on. But the presence within us, the observer of all that is, contains nothing in and of itself. It's merely a conscious observer. And in that nothingness there can exist neither end of the polarity.

Try it for yourself. Sit still. Focus on your breathing. As thoughts enter in, just acknowledge them and then simply allow them to float away like clouds in the sky. Then ask yourself the question, 'what is here for me right now?'. If you find yourself associating with what is being observed, just return to your breath and cycle through the practice again until all you are left with is the nothingness of pure observation, pure awareness.

Polarities dictate that there can be no good without bad; no laughter without sorrow. This is why striving for happiness as an end in itself will not work, because attached to that happiness is its polarity. Polarities are always attached in some way to their opposite. Just think about some polarities for a minute and consider if any of them could exist without their opposite:

- negative and positive
- light and dark
- good and evil
- masculine and feminine
- interior and exterior
- stability and change
- competition and collaboration
- beginning and end
- part and whole
- left and right
- up and down
- active and passive

Hence the only way to free ourselves from either end of a polarity is to free ourselves from the entire energy of the duality that is inherent in the polarity. We can't force into life any single end of a polarity because it's still attached to its opposite. Happiness therefore isn't something that is forced, that we can create in and of itself; it is the spiritual energy that flows when we return to our natural state, when we return to nothingness.

So if it's about nothingness, then why do we have an entire chapter devoted to 'you'? We have another truth at work that is wrapped up in a paradox. Whilst the awareness, the consciousness that is you is essentially immaterial in nature (hence the quality of 'nothingness') that doesn't mean that you have no 'being' as a person. This dimension is therefore about understanding the 'being-ness' that is you - the heart of you; the highest version of you that is fully open to endless possibility and limitless power.

If the 'you' at the centre of all of this is not open to flow, is struggling with egoic misconceptions, is in a state of stress, or has some kind of messianic or heroic view of your mission as a leader, then none of this will work. Understand the 'everything' and then the nothing will come into play, that is, when you hook into the truth of who or what you are and how that feeds into your role as a leader, then start practising Transcendent Leadership, you will find that the appearance of nothingness will begin to manifest. People will not see you huffing and puffing, working all hours, running on cortisol. They will feel your influence, your presence, and they will feel better for it, even if they don't quite know why. When this happens, you will know what it feels like to be practising leadership at Level Three, at the level of Transcendence.

****

Remember the teaching I mentioned earlier? 'The greatest gift we can give our clients is the *Absolute Certainty* that they already have everything that they need to be who they need to be.' What sits at the heart of this truth? For me it's connection. One person's soul connecting with another person's soul. The American pastor and writer, John C. Maxwell once said, "Leadership is not about titles, positions, or flow charts. It is about one life influencing another." This is when we as a person are able to know with Absolute Certainty that the people that we lead can and will achieve what they set out to, or to even go beyond their original aspirations. It is then that we are truly manifesting our own personal mastery as a leader.

But first you need to make that shift in your own identification in the journey from Second to Third Level. So I would invite you to pause for a minute or two and consider the following 'identification questions':
Who are you?
Why are you a leader?
Was it planned or did it happen through circumstance?
Where is your investment? Are you invested fully in leadership or do you just put up with it?
Where is the ego in all of this?
Where should it be?
Are the latter two answers the same for you?

In striving for Third Level understanding of leadership, identification is such an important component to grasp. Much has been made of the heroic leader in the last couple of decades. Many commentators suggest that the day of the heroic leader – the charismatic, thrusting, willy-waving executive, is over. Look around you. It's really not. Maybe it should be, but the heroic leader is still alive and well. I was actually informally coaching a traumatised senior manager just yesterday after an encounter with just such a person recently.

So look critically at yourself. If you are heavily invested in your status, your own self-importance, and if you have a personal ego-stake in the outcome of your team or organisation, then you have some work to do to make the radical jump up to Third Level. So many people are in leadership positions out of a sense of duty, because of what their parents expected of them, of fate, or merely circumstance. It may be due to being the most qualified person around, or it might be for money or to satisfy a desire for status or self-importance. If it is any of these things that have pushed you into a leadership position, reflect on them honestly and if you're serious about making the shift upwards, then work on them with all earnestness.

It may be that you are teetering on the edge of Second Level, and you can almost touch Third Level, you can begin to see it in outline, you can feel what it might be like. Then open yourself to the truths in this book. You will know when you have arrived because you will feel it deep within. Nobody can tell you if you have got there. When you make the shift, you will experience that dramatic change within and without. Your light will shine more brightly, people will notice, but it is you who are the ultimate authority of this revelation. Shifting to Level Three is a bit like falling in love for the first time. Before falling in love, you might have read about it or seen it in movies, but you only know its power when you experience it. Then you're in no doubt that you've arrived.

When you make the shift in consciousness that will take you through to Third Level, you will come to realise that it was only by opening up to something bigger than you, let's call it spiritual or mystical wisdom, and it is that which will carry you on wings of angels up to the highest levels. Your very persona as a leader will rest on eternal truth and justice and knowledge. Sure, you will continue to have to write left-brain informed business plans and suchlike. But the new truth that you hold, the 'downloads' that you receive, will not be based on reasoning. No, this truth must be discerned spiritually, because it comes from a different place. When you reach this point, you will know that you have transcended the Second Level.

When you do so, you will then be prepared to open up to coming into full alignment with your mission. When you wake up to the divine being inside of you, you also awaken to your life's truest purpose. In a sense, that's what the two halves of the dimensions in this book are all about. The first half of the book, the foundational dimensions, is all about deep healing work – when we move beyond past hurts and misconceptions of self, in order to wake to the divinity within. The second half, the cyclical dimensions, are the transformational work – connecting with your true genius and then giving it away.

Some people spend a lifetime on the spiritual path, only going inwards, a lifetime of introspection and taking from spirit and other people. Some people never make the inward connection and spend a lifetime just giving, or just working, but they come from a place of disconnection, of automatic conditioning. In our awakened state, we recognise the duality in this and seek to reconcile it. It's not one nor the other. One cannot come to full realisation without the other. The awakened being who is not also giving of their gifts is an empty vessel. The unawakened being who is giving but doing so in their own strength will not realise their full potential because everything comes *from* them; nothing flows *through* them.

Fortunately in the both/and universe of the Third Level leader, we combine both to miraculous effect. But the foundation is a healthy, conscious identification of self. So let us first have a look at examples of unhealthy identification as a leader, and use these insights to help us to define the healthy zone in which a Transcendent Leader might operate.

Everybody connects internally and externally using a set of programs. In their basic state, we can say that we operate using ten digits in the decimal numeral system plus in English we use the 26 letters of the alphabet. These combine to create language and maths. I'd encourage you to have a look at my review of Ken Wilber's 'Superhuman Operating System' on YouTube. The Operating System is based upon Wilber's model of the person, both internally and externally. It is essentially a map, a theory of everything in the human condition throughout time. The map includes history, philosophy, religion, anthropology, systems such as economics, psychology, politics and so on. In so doing, Wilber encompasses the totality of matter, soul, spirit, mind and body into an holistic network that forms the map.

The Superhuman Operating System is a course of study as well as self-reflection. Firstly we understand the map. The map consists of lines and levels of intelligence or development. There are also quadrants, holons and stages. All of these aspects of the map describe the matrix of being within which we operate. Like the movie, The Matrix, we are trapped inside it until we open our eyes and see the matrix for the first time. When we see it and understand it, this understanding is in itself psycho-active in nature. i.e. the knowledge filters over time into your conscious and sub-conscious and the very structure of your mind changes as a result.

Within the practice of Awakening Coaching, the coach is always on the look-out for these underlying programs that have entered the sub-conscious. Such programs can remain hidden until revealed by the coach. Once revealed, however, the client can often see for the first time just how powerful and perfidious these programs have been in their life. The task is then to release or dissolve the programs and to bring the client back to natural presence.

On the socio-psychological level, we are absolutely riddled with these programs which underlie many of our often hidden beliefs and assumptions. The programs then form the filter through which we judge inputs and formulate outputs. They can absolutely drive our lives without our being aware of them.

Let me give you an example. A common unhealthy program that is running in the background of many leaders is one of insecurity. The insecure person puts their insecurities out into the world; their personal 'output' is coloured or filtered through the prism of insecurity. If a leader has programs associated with insecurity running in their mind, then they handicap themselves in how they connect with people.

This is a major problem - people want *more* engagement in the workplace; people naturally feel good when they're fully engaged. However, if engagement is filtered through insecurity, then creativity and flow and connection is smothered because authentic communication simply cannot be established.

Thus faulty programs create insecurities, the insecurities create a barrier to such leaders in being able to fully reveal who they are to the workforce, and this in turn creates a block to engagement. The lack of engagement pushes 'followers' away, which in turn creates more insecurity and thus a negative feedback loop is created.

Awareness or intra-personal intelligence is therefore the key to solving the problem of the unconscious programming of the mind. Indeed, the mind is a palimpsest in which you see all the layers and messy tangles of one's life. Without awareness, untangling it and discerning all the different strands of conditioning and programming is all but impossible. Most people running these programs are entirely unaware of the fact that they have been installed, hard-wired into the mind, thus forming the design of the internal human operating system.

Such people can be unconsciously driven by the unencumbered ego. They use the ego in a position of leadership to drive their egoic power-base. In the West, this has often been magnified as the notion of the collective has been somewhat lost in the pursuit of individualism, and the idea of the heroic leader has been glamorised. The model of the heroic leader is fuel to the unencumbered ego.

As well as increasing our self-awareness, we can also begin to transcend the poor mind-wiring and unhelpful programming by moving our focus away from 'self' and towards that which we lead, i.e. our ambition shifts from centring on self-advancement to advancement of that which our organisation is designed to deliver, be it goods, services, charity or whatever. When we do this, we trigger a powerful shift that brings us towards 'transcendence' as a leader.

But to go even deeper and to bring greater healing, we need to work on the much more fundamental level of the mind itself, which forms the core of our operating system. The mind is an amazing thing. We often think of our mind as a great tool, in fact possibly the greatest tool that we have – the thing that distinguishes us from the animal kingdom. The mind created everything on this planet that is great about humanity. It created art, culture, architecture, philosophy, human rights, concepts of liberty and so on. But the mind also creates everything that is bad – war, conflict, racism.

Whether used for good or for bad, for most of us most of the time, we unknowingly don't really use the mind, rather the mind uses *us!* This is the disease that cannot easily be shaken. The mind has taken over its master – it is not *our* slave, *we* are the slave to the mind due to the delusion created by the mind that we are our job, our curriculum vitae, our relationships, our abilities and so on. Of course we can relate to these things, but our mind takes it all too far, to the point were we are unconsciously identified with the mind to such a degree that we cannot see that it is our master, to the point were most people are completely unable to reach for the button to switch it off.

The mind is a machine of almost infinite activity, most of which is simply wasteful or indeed, positively harmful. This mind activity is based upon the conscious and sub-conscious programs that are running in the background. The main underlying program, the operating system that controls all programs, therefore, creates the illusion that the mind is who or what we truly are. Installed on this operating program are the main software programs.

Typical programs are based on beliefs. We often form these beliefs early on in life. Examples are:
- I'm not good enough
- I'll always be poor
- Nobody loves me
- There's not enough time
- People are judging me
- Life is a struggle

Maybe take a few moments and feel into these beliefs. Are there any that resonate for you? What has been installed as your own personal operating system? Are you truly neutral and free from any of these? Be very suspicious of a positive answer to the latter question – I have never come across anybody who hasn't got any beliefs deeply installed and which act as drivers to thoughts and actions. If you come up with nothing, maybe talk it through with somebody who knows you very well.

I was reminded the other day of the truth that once we dissolve these unhelpful programs, we come to the realisation that actually we're all of the same essence under the surface. At the most fundamental level, our true nature is just awareness. It is simply consciousness.

Consider these statements for a moment:
- You have a body, but you are not your body
- You have feelings, but you are not your feelings
- You have possessions, but you are not your possessions
- You have thoughts, but you are not your thoughts
- You have a history, but you are not your history

Get it? See, it's simple. The truth is that you are just the thing that is aware of all of these things. That's the reason that even for people that are objectively rather old, they often say that they don't feel old. That's entirely true, because the part of you that you identify with deep down is simply this awareness that lies outside of space and time. The real you is the observer of it all: it sees but cannot be seen, because it has no size, no shape, no beginning and no end. Some people refer to this as your spirit or your soul. It is the awareness that sits behind all that is manifest.

This awareness has no body, no substance. Our spirit, our consciousness, has no form. It is no-thing, or nothing. As I explained a few pages ago, this is our natural state. If we identify with or as anything, then this is simply a lie created by the mind and automatic conditioning.

I was reminded of this the other day – the great leveller that is the ultimate truth of our existence – that outward appearances, the body, what we own and so on, are not the real 'me'. I was with my family in a wonderful place called Cotehele in Cornwall, when we decided to pose for a photograph on a thing I called a 'horse mounty steppy thing' (correctly known as a 'mounting block'). And we all magically became the same height:

My five year old stood on the top step; then the thirteen year old; then the fifteen year old. Finally me, on the ground. It made me recognise that under all of the outer manifestation, and all of the inner programming, we are all the same. Standing as we did, all of our heights became one in alignment. Suddenly one of the great outer differentiators between us disappeared. Within us, all is the same, merely awareness, just this nothingness I spoke about above. All of us start from the same place when all is stripped away. When we are able to recognise this anew everyday and learn to stand aside for Spirit to do its work in our mission, that's the beginning of wisdom.

Before I move on, just a note about this 'nothingness'. Some people, particularly those prone to 'spiritual bypassing' or those who dedicate their life to blissing out in spirit, are advocates of the notion that the 'ground of being' is pure consciousness or even nothingness itself. Some develop this idea and say that we are in fact holograms, and that all experience is illusion. This is a leadership book, not a philosophical treatise, however, it's worth just briefly explicating and contextualising what I see as the broad ground of being upon which Transcendent Leadership practice sits.

Any practice has to be based upon something, some kind of an understanding or belief. In the thrusting, 'yuppie' dominated 1980s, leadership was based upon a strong sense of individualism, of power and accumulation. Millennials and then Gen-Zers shifted the dialogue on towards a more holistic view of life which meant that leaders had to respond in kind with a more emotional, empathetic set of skills.

Even as society shifts in this way, there has to be something upon which the philosophy of leadership ultimately sits. The thing that I refer to above as the 'ground of being' is that which is left when everything else is stripped away. The problem in finding a landing spot on this ground is that we are reliant upon language to explain it, and language is not reality, it is merely an abstraction of reality.

What I am fairly certain about, however, is that 'nothingness' is not the ground of reality. It is a reasonable way to describe consciousness as consciousness is devoid of matter. But we can't leave it at that in my opinion - life has more meaning than that. There is no meaning in pure consciousness, pure nothingness. So what is the range of possibility? Eastern philosophies often indeed suggest that the ground of being is consciousness; western religion would suggest that it's God. Atheists that it is stuff - material. Maybe it's all three?

What occurs to me is that the eastern philosophies are potentially at risk of reductionism which is the criticism aimed at atheists. The latter suggest that ultimately life is just a soup of particles and molecules hence lacks any meaning. My issue is that if we do the same and reach the conclusion that ultimately we are no 'thing', just pure consciousness, isn't this then reductionism as well? Where is the meaning in this?

The second law of thermodynamics, entropy, would suggest that everything should be becoming more chaotic over time. However, when we observe the cosmos, we actually see more and more order and more complexity and more beauty developing over time. Maybe this is because the ground of being is something more than pure consciousness or pure material. A friend of mine, Don MacGregor, who wrote the foreword to this book, was discussing this with me, and suggested therefore that the ground of being is borne of this informational field. He put it to me thus:

"Some scientists are saying that the basic level, below that of energy, is one of informational patterns, acted on by universal mind or consciousness, to form a holographic universe that follows the same patterns throughout. Everything is interconnected in this vast network of interdependent energies formed from the informational field. The material world as we know it stems or emanates from a deeper level of information like a universal mind. And that all form, all material matter, has its origin in mind or consciousness. From a scientific viewpoint, the whole universe is the out-picturing of a cosmic consciousness. This is the beginning of the coming together of science and spirituality. As one person said in comment on this, 'It is now rational to be spiritual!'"

If the field of information is cosmic consciousness, then maybe it's not too much of a leap to say that this consciousness has some concern for the cosmos, that it's not a merely dispassionate consciousness. So perhaps the ground of being is actually love and if love comes from God and God is love, then maybe the two are inseparable, i.e. intimately intertwined. They are holarchic in nature, i.e. love does not *come* from God – love *is* God. Similarly, God does not *come* from love God *is* love. I wonder if God-Love is the ground of being? Maybe God-Love is one and the same as cosmic consciousness, just expressed differently?

I put this to an orthodox fundamentalist friend who reacted rather negatively to the notion. Western religious thought won't much like the notion that love and God are holarchic - This is counter to the general love of dualism in the west – separation between creator and created and so on.

Another friend of mine, the African missionary, John Walters, told me, "Both the one logical objective answer and one logical subjective answer are inherent within the question. Consciousness is a prerequisite for even posing the question. If we postulate that there is no actual creator God, but only a human construct, then ALL alternatives derive from consciousness. So consciousness is the only logical objective answer."

He went on, "However if a creator God does exist, which cannot be rigorously demonstrated objectively, then God would be the originator of consciousness and therefore the ground of all human experience....the very ground of existence. As a trained research scientist (in the distant past) I like to work within the realms of objectivity. But that training also highlights the limits of objectivity. My experience of God cannot be explained objectively so I bow to my (subjectively perceived) God and recognise him as the ground of my existence. This is the only logical answer to the question when all considerations are taken into account."

I think that I can therefore say for certain that the ground of being remains something of a mystery. However, I am increasingly certain that I am not drawn to the reductionist 'nothingness/consciousness' answer as it carries with it no purpose. Everything I know about life seems to carry with it some kind of purpose. Broadly, I favour the notion that the ground is God-Love and probably actually God-Love-Information. We might also refer to God-Love as Spirit. This imbues the ground of being and hence your life with meaning and purpose. The Operating System upon which Spirit sits as it were, is energetic informational patterns that operate within a field of consciousness. Without this field of information, entropy would take over and the cosmos would become more and more dysfunctional, but this is not what we observe, hence the need for Information to be included within the ground of being.

This is important in that the Transcendent Leader works from and within this field of Spirit-Information, it is the underpinning operating system upon which all the seeming magic emerges. Downloads, inspiration, creativity, synchronicities, coherence - they do not come from nothing. They emerge from this infinitely powerful source, the ground of all being.

The Transcendent Leader is thus on a journey to recognising and bringing back control over the programs that have been piled high on top of this field of Spirit-Information. Recognition that the programs are indeed there is the first step. We then ask if the programs are helpful or unhelpful. If they are unhelpful to us, I have developed some beautiful, simple but incredibly powerful tools that dissolve these programs and the stranglehold that they have over our lives. You can find such practices in my book, Mind-Spirit Detox that are designed to do just this.

Unlike Mind-Spirit Detox, this book is not specifically about practices. However, I have included in this book many pointers and reflections which direct us towards the truth of who or what you really are; truths that allow that which is bigger than us to enter into our leadership practice and the habits that drive that practice.

Just remember another guiding truth, though, which is that whilst you have to move beyond the egoic self, the 'small *you*', there is still very much a 'you' at play here. This 'you' has to be fully brought in to the mission that sits behind the practice. This is where authenticity comes into play. In order for the real 'you' to step forwards as a leader, you must first step into the authentic 'self'. You have to define and *re*fine your aspiration.

Ask yourself what you want. What is it that you *really* want? If you fail to clarify this basic point, then your intentions will remain opaque and undefined. This is problematic because Spirit cannot work with a divided or unfocussed will. But when you connect with the singularity of desire when you become fully cognisant of who or what you are and what you are about in your walk on the planet, then Spirit comes flooding in and energises you in your journey towards your own True North. That's what it means to be your authentic self at Level Three.

We're not playing around here or pretending or acting a part. It's as real and absolute as it can be or the whole thing just does not work. Inner unification that comes about when you establish clarity over what you genuinely want produces a powerful peace of knowing and a direction, guided by Spirit that carries you with an arrow-sharp precision towards your goal.

This will then be brilliantly noticeable by those that you lead in terms of the behaviours that you display. Having said that, I actually rarely talk about behaviours in my leadership practice. Some trainers in the field of management and organisational development drone on endlessly about behaviours, but in my experience, it is one of the least fruitful of all training/development subjects. That is because behaviour is merely a symptom; an outward manifestation of belief, driven by what resides in the head and the heart. Without the hard work and long journey of waking up and growing up associated with development at this most profound of levels, you're frankly wasting your time. Do the work, however, get alignment between head, heart and clarity of direction, and then when you cast your eyes around, you will see an army of followers. Your very being, your life, is the thing that does the leading. Let your true nature be the example to others.

> "If you would convince a man that he does wrong, do right. But do not care to convince him. Men will believe what they see. Let them see."
>
> *Henry David Thoreau*

So how do we come into presence and begin to notice our internal programs in order to stand a chance of turning this around? How are we to bring our best selves to the leadership arena? When we operate from a position of transcendence, how does this manifest? How do we shift away from ego in our journey towards transcendence? How do we live out our mission as a divine being? How do we fully allow the Universe to manifest good within the people's lives who we lead, and into whatever it is that we seek to create? Is it even possible to re-program our internal operating system?

This is where the notion of 'service' comes in. The lightbulb moment for many people is when they recognise that they themselves gain so much more by *giving* as a leader. This is when many people begin to transcend the selfish ego drive that can be present in leadership at lower levels.

We need to recognise the disease of the glorification of self, the individuated 'me', that pervades Western thought. When we make the sense of self more opaque and focus instead on the collective and what we can do to serve that collective, then we begin to transcend outmoded models of leadership. When we do so we overcome, move beyond, and shift to the next level. That's where the magic begins to happen, because the self is no longer acting as a barrier to what the Universe wants to manifest through us.

We need to be very careful however, not to see this as a logical trade-off, or trade-up. If we decide to start giving rather than receiving purely because when we give, we ultimately get more back, then we're still using ego and we are operating on the mind-thought plane. Indeed, it could be seen as a cynical exercise in manipulation. So again, we need to transcend this level of transaction.

The difference between a Transcendent Leader and an ego-driven leader comes down to love and compassion, two words that you won't find very often in the literature around leadership. If it is all about love and compassion, of course the self still exists, but the difference is that it fades into the background; it isn't important any longer. And as and when the ego pops back up, as it surely will, our job is to recognise it and deal with it. I will invite you to reflect for yourself upon the meaning of love and compassion in your own leadership journey. Do these two words carry with them any resonance in the context of your own practice? Is there something holding you back? What steps might you take to unblock the flow of love and compassion?

A brilliant example of the principle of giving is a South American retreat I have stayed in with my family called Marianela, which is located in some beautiful jungle-clad hills. The head priest, known as the "Paí", is part of a movement called the Redemptorists. He is an Italian missionary who was called to South America in his early 20s. One night he had a dream about setting up a retreat in the countryside. In the dream, he was told the scale of the place (big!), what it would look like, how to go about building it and so on. The next day, he rang his main contact in Rome, an Italian Cardinal, and told him all about the dream, in every detail. After he related the story, the Paí thought that the Cardinal would tell him that he was mad, that it was just a dream, and that he should let it go. However, the Paí told me that the Cardinal paused for a few long moments, and then simply said, 'well, we'd better make this happen, then!'. Soon afterwards, the Paí met with the Cardinal in Rome, who took him on a tour of wealthy Catholic friends in Italy and in a few short weeks, he had enough money and pledges of support to buy the land and start to build the retreat.

A detailed interview with this remarkable man can be found in the blog section of www.awakeningcoaching.co.uk. The point here, however, is that the Paí was a man absolutely operating beyond the ego. He said that the church in Rome is very driven by power and ego and politics, which contrasts strongly with his view of Jesus as a quiet revolutionary, driven by love and compassion. And in terms of his own mission, here is a man who has created the most amazing and really quite massive retreat centre, who has planted tens of thousands of native trees, who has a working organic farm and who has brought a vision of love and hope to thousands of people. He never for one minute doubted that the vision would be manifest, because never for one minute was any of this about *him*. As such, the Universe flowed abundantly through him. Humility was at its heart and therefore that same humility is what allowed power to flow. When you look into the Paí's eyes, you look straight into his soul. The power and creativity and the Absolute Certainty you see in his eyes is profound, and the driving force behind it all is love and compassion.

> "I have three precious things which I hold fast and prize. The first is gentleness; the second is frugality; the third is humility, which keeps me from putting myself before others. Be gentle and you can be bold; be frugal and you can be liberal; avoid putting yourself before others and you can become a leader among men."
>
> *Lao Tzu*

So here is a compass question: Do you believe in a cause that is bigger than you? What out there is just wanting to flow through you? Are you yourself standing in its way? If you already are working on such a cause or mission, is your ego acting as a barrier to its manifestation?

If you're struggling still with ego, do not focus too much on it. People for millennia have tried and failed to overcome the ego. By attempting to subvert it or destroy it, you will expend a huge amount of energy in so doing and results are hard to come by. Instead, try focussing on the mission, on your team and the things you need to do to manifest that mission. Then, the self, the ego, will fade away into the background and begin to dissolve. It won't do so completely, but if and when it should arise in an unhelpful way, acknowledge it and move on.

Another way to think about this is to recognise that the Universe will flow through you in abundance when you don't make it about yourself. Leadership can often be associated with glamour – be that in status, power, possessions, charisma. But those people who transcend the old paradigms are those who do not seek to self-glamorise. Greatness comes to people who focus their mission away from themselves.

So to summarise, the paradox plays out thus: If we make our mission in the world about 'me', in the mistaken belief that this is the way to advance our career, populate the CV etc. then we are coming from a position of 'lack', i.e. the 'me' in all of this is really quite small, it begins at your feet and ends at the top of your head.

Of course, there is a mind, there is a mouth, there are your accumulated skills and knowledge, but it is still just a thing called 'me'. If we picture this 'me', or the ego, as a gate, then imagine that you open the gate to the universe. The gate, i.e. the me/ego still exists, but it is open, it is getting out of the way. And now the leadership resource is immediately transformed, indeed, transcended, from the small 'me' into the infinite abundance of the universe. We move from the finite, i.e. me within my own ambition for *me*, towards the infinite realm of endless possibility, i.e. me as a conduit for the ambition of the universe.

One of the key shift points in the third dimension of becoming the true 'you' is to understand the process by which we can become this conduit for the universe. For some people who are already in leadership positions, this can be the most problematic hurdle to overcome.

Many people in leadership roles have had a history of success, either academic, technical, professional, or entrepreneurial. With that goes quite some degree of self-confidence, or at the very least, compensatory bluster; an outward show of confidence. At its very basic level, people who hadn't ever had much ambition to be a leader may achieve leadership just thanks to their inherent ability in a particular area. I had a colleague who was in a middle management position. He wasn't particularly ambitions, in fact, he really wasn't ambitious at all. He told me that he had reached his level of moderate seniority merely because he was good at what he did. He said, 'don't ever think about where you want to get to; if you're good enough, you'll naturally rise up to a decent enough place'.

For me, this is **Unconscious Surrender**, or the first stage. This is the level where we are just what we are. We are just doing what everybody else seemingly does. Just living our normal life, doing what is expected, not recognising anything beyond the mundane, the inane even.

What proportion of the population live at this level? To some degree, quite possibly nearly all of the population, certainly it has to be up around the 75% plus mark. This is the level where we are effectively asleep at the wheel, where we do not recognise that the thoughts that we have are creating the reality that we see around us. The fact is that our internal world creates our external reality and most people do not recognise this. In fact, it's probably akin to the conversation between goldfish: Goldfish #1, 'what do you think of the water today?'; Goldfish #2, 'what water?!'

The second stage is **Conscious Control**, i.e. the antithesis of the first stage. People coming into leadership roles from a more expansive perspective may have consciously shifted into their own power, they may have a notion of their greatness, their deepest longing, their genius, and have therefore learnt to take control of thoughts and feelings, and have simultaneously learnt how to dampen down doubt and hence begin the road to self-realisation and manifestation of their dreams, and to consciously create their own lives.

For many people, this appears to be the highest form of being. It is referenced in the New Thought movement, which holds that our mental states are carried forward into manifestation and become our experience in daily living. Many people in the higher consciousness movement or spiritually aware people have made it their daily practice to live within this realm. There are many popular podcasts/radio shows that profess this type of outlook, such as Peter Tongue's 'Awakening to Conscious Co-Creation'.

The Conscious Control level holds that our internal environment is actually contributing to how the external environment presents itself; internal belief creates external reality. This level is a world away from the Unconscious Surrender level. At the Conscious Control level, we wake up to the fact that we are a creative being, and that we can be a little bit more in charge of how our life unfolds. We recognise that our thoughts can have an impact on the reality around us and our lived experience on this planet. This stage brings with it a sense of power, of self-actualisation, of empowerment and of creativity.

For those who are new to this notion, try this practice:

- Day 1: consciously be grumpy and short with everybody you encounter. Do not smile, think negative thoughts, feel into worst case scenarios. Give off negativity at every opportunity.

What happens? What comes back to you? How did that day unfold?

- Day 2: banish negative thoughts; breathe deeply, ground yourself, smile, laugh. Ask people how they are, connect deeply with those around you. Tell your family that you love them. Be creative. Live in the moment.

How was that? How did it compare with Day 1?

There can be no clearer way to see the reality that lies behind the Conscious Control level. It's so demonstrable that we get back what we give out. The New Thought movement explains it thus: 'thoughts held in mind produce after their kind'.

So far so good. Moving from Unconscious Surrender to Conscious Control is a revolution in being, it is truly a conscious shift from being a victim of life's circumstance, a passive passenger on an unscripted journey, towards being a fully realized driver of the train. The difference is one of night and day.

However, those that make the mistake of thinking that this train has now arrived at the station are monumentally wrong, because there is a further level of being, that of **Conscious Surrender.** At this level, we move beyond the paradigm of placing ourselves in the all-powerful centre of our own story, and we begin to recognise that there is something outside and inside of us, i.e. something that **transcends** us. We might call it 'spirit', or 'what is', or 'the cosmos', 'Big Mind', or even 'God'. Whatever we call it, it has the properties of the infinite, the divine, of a mind or an order bigger than but containing the small 'us'. This divine force is continually working through us and with us on behalf of both us as individuals and us as a collective body.

As you explore your role as leader, I would invite you to be open and curious and excited about what Conscious Surrender might feel like to you. Take a moment or two to contemplate the new worlds that this might open up for you, your team and your organisation as you truly stand on the edge of infinite creative possibility.

When you break through into Third Level, it feels like breaking through a layer of cloud in an airliner as you rise higher and higher. Above the cloud – clear skies, infinitely vast. This is where the cruising altitude of your life can be attained, where creativity and manifestation of your deepest longing occurs in a seemingly effortless space.

In the words of Adyashanti,

> "As you come into harmony in life, then mysteriously, also miraculously, life seems to come into harmony with you. There is a sense

> that everything is unfolding just as it needs to, that everything is right on time. As we let go of trying to control life, trying to force in the direction that the ego wants it to go, life has a way of literally responding to our state of consciousness and that's a miracle – that as your state of consciousness transforms, life's relationship with you transforms as well."
>
> Adyashanti, Resurrecting Jesus

Try to tune in to where you are. Reflect on the stage you are at. If you are still operating at ground level, how much do you desire to break through that cloud layer and surrender up that personal, human control, to the higher spirit, to the divine?

To pass through the clouds into the big sky beyond takes courage and curiosity. The truth is that neither you nor I know what lies beyond those clouds. It can even be terrifying for some, because it's opening up new horizons, new territory. It's an entirely new expansion for anyone to do this. We do not know what might want to come through us. But that's the excitement!

What I can say for certain that the nature of what will come through you will be LOVE! If you truly desire to channel the 'good' that is already there for you, then whatever comes through will be carried on the vibration of love. There will be knowing, there will be alignment. The force that works through you will feel just right, it will feel like a coming home to the true 'you'. Synchronicities will begin to flow, of such magnitude that they feel like miracles.

Note that you cannot just skip straight up to the level of Conscious Surrender. It's a learning process, and as with every learning process, you don't just jump to the last chapter. Each stage is built upon the conditions created by the previous stage. And in each stage, you don't simply throw away the previous one. Nothing is destroyed, rather, it is contained within the next stage. Furthermore, moving into each stage isn't like a one-way valve. It's more nuanced and mercurial than that. Understanding, practice and learning ebbs and flows on its journey through the levels.

There are plentiful parts of each of my days where I'm operating from First Stage. Then I might break the spell somehow and shift into Second Stage. I may then recognise that I'm going round in circles in my own power and getting nowhere, so I consciously surrender up my efforts and shift up to Third Level, letting Spirit take control. Thus it's a fluid process and we have to recognise that we inhabit many different levels, like an aeroplane in flight, there are various different altitudes we can fly at in any one day.

Another way of looking at this is to consider the conditions by which ecosystems develop. Supposing you have an eruption of magma in a place such as the Mid-Atlantic Rift. On 14th November 1963, Surtsey, an island off the coast of Iceland, appeared as if from nowhere. It was formed by a volcanic eruption beginning on the sea bed, 130 metres down. At its peak, it spanned one square mile. Within a couple of years, the first vascular plant was seen. Soon, mosses and lichens appeared. Then fungi. Soon, these plants created the conditions for birds to begin to visit. They helped soil conditions to improve, which in turn created the conditions for the first bush to appear. Each stage creates the necessary conditions for the emergence of the next stage. As we continue, grasslands might emerge, then trees, then forests. Eventually the ecosystem will flourish, with a rich web of interdependent life. However, in the same way as an ecosystem can consist of all stages of bio-colonisation, i.e. fungi, mosses and trees can co-exist and remain co-dependent, so, too, do the three key stages of leadership remain in a co-existent partnership.

The important point here is that we cannot simply jump straight to the forest. Each stage is a necessary precursor to the next. In the same way, it is simply not possible to pass from the 'transactional' stage, Level One, straight through to the transcendent stage, Level Three. First we need to understand what the transformational stage has to offer; to understand how, through our own efforts, through the understanding of motivation and strategy formation, we are able to transform teams and products.

It is simply not possible as a leader in the real world to exist in a bubble of transcendence. At all times, the transactional and transformational activities of leadership and management must continue. Without an accounting function, an ordering function, a business relationship function and a product development and delivery function, all activities that reside firmly in the lower two levels, transcendence is frankly vacuous. After all, a tree cannot exist without the soil; soil must come before the tree. Likewise, Levels One and Two must exist before Level Three can manifest in your practice. Therefore you absolutely must still have team objectives, cascaded from organisational objectives and strategy; you must monitor performance through Key Performance Indicators and Balanced Scorecards and so on. Level Three will only succeed if Levels Two and One are also present in your practice.

Whilst on the issue of objectives and KPIs, however, the Level Three Leader has a rather more enlightened attitude around these matters. I once heard somebody say, 'you don't get a pig fatter by weighing it all the time'. Likewise, the person who wants to lose weight doesn't do so by having a daily weigh-in. The way to achieve things is to set an outcome as something that you want to create that isn't yet manifest. The next stage is to work out the levers available to you to realise the outcome, e.g. what are the habits that you need to regularly practise to bring this about? Then focus all of your energy on these habits. You can pretty much forget about the outcome because if you've shifted the focus of your daily habits in the right way, the outcome will emerge.

The notion of being ruthlessly focussed on outcomes is a seductive one but it is one doomed to failure. The fruit of your input will emerge of its own accord if your inputs are set correctly. We can be attached to the inputs but we need to let the outcomes look after themselves.

In the Bhagavad Gita, non-attachment to outcomes is called, 'Karma Yoga', the path of 'consecrated action'. It is a wonderful way to remove personal striving and inner stress from desired external outcomes. When we remove the inner fractured energy in this way, we open ourselves and the situation to universal energetic flow. As a result, desired outcomes manifest more readily and with less personal effort because as with everything at Level Three, we are opening up to the energy of the

Cosmos, we're not doing everything using our own humble resources.

This was brought home to me some time ago when discussing a job opportunity with a colleague who used to work in my team and who moved away. He had achieved promotion and desperately wanted to return to my team because of its positivity, innovation and cultural 'vibe'. I spoke with him about Transcendent Leadership, a concept that he very much embraced. However, he said that there was no way in which he would be able to practise this in his current team. This was because the conditions were not right. They were barely getting the transactional processes right, let alone the transformational. For him to attempt to practice Transcendent Leadership in this environment would have been futile, like plonking a tree down on the early Surtsey island.

The fluidity between the Levels is also down to the role of the ego. The ego does one of two things. It either falsely tells you that you are incredible, the most amazing thing that ever happened to planet earth and those around you. Or it tells you that you are nothing, worthless, useless. 'You are nobody to be doing these things', it often says.

The response has to be, 'who am I NOT to do these things?!'. Keep this in mind when you first make the shift to Third Level, because this is the moment at which the latter, contracting ego, sometimes makes its presence felt. This might be because there are only three stages involved. Therefore, necessarily, there is an enormous gulf between each of the stages. They are literally like different universes. Each one is built on the proceeding one; each stage is therefore totally necessary to your growth, like a springboard into the next universe. When you have made that shift into the next universe, there is a part of you that will be utterly taken, driven, excited and absorbed by this.

The ego however, might take some time to catch up. It often feels like there's a tether back into the previous universe, the previous stage. The journey in Third Level is of such an order of magnitude different to that in Level One and Level Two that our small mind can often be overwhelmed. It's a bit like being on a roller coaster. It's exhilarating, but a part of you just wants it to be over and to get back down to terra firma, where things feel safe and familiar.

So do not be surprised if your small mind (the ego) plonks you back down into First Stage or Second Stage during the day or even for days or weeks on end. The key, however, is to reconnect with Source. Remind yourself of the bigger picture and your role in it. Have a look at the chapters, 'Die to Self', and 'Heaven is Here!' in my book, Mind-Spirit Detox for practices to expand your field of view, and where you fit in, also a great practice to reincarnate, to throw off the small self.

The key to this is awareness. Be conscious of what stage you are operating from at any given moment. You will never realistically be operating from Third Level all of the time. But you can practice bouncing back up into this stage and the more you do it, the more you will connect with spirit, with the ego-less real 'self' and the more natural it will become. Flow is like an energy that feeds off itself. The more you get up into the cruising altitude of Third Level, the more the natural energy of the Universe flows through you and the more flow this attracts. It's a bit like rolling a snowball to make a snowman. The bigger the snowball gets, the more snow it attracts. It becomes an exponential rush of energy.

A wonderful practice that you can engage at any point to ensure that you are in awareness is to bring yourself to the present moment. To be fully engaged with the moment that we call 'now'. Focus on your breathing. The breath in and the breath out and the momentary pause between one and the other can only be experienced in the present moment. Thoughts of the past and of the future are entirely unreal, the stuff of our imagination. That's why the past and the future is the domain of the ego. The ego is always seeking to make sense of the past in terms of self-identification. It projects into the future in an endless cycle variously of lack and of ambition.

The present moment that can be attained through breath-work is the key to self-liberation because it is the only moment in which the true self can be present. Whenever you are in your mind, you cannot connect with the present and your true self is in deficit because it does not exist in the mind. So connect with the breath as often as you can and ask yourself, 'what is here?'. It is the key to awakening and de-programming. It is the starting place for a re-boot of your entire system to become the best version of you...the radical redesign of the perfect you as the ultimate leader for the mission that lies out ahead of you.

Thus to summarise the third dimension of Transcendent Leadership: By consciously surrendering your egoic self, you open up to becoming one with your true nature and by so doing, shift beyond autonomic programming and create the inner conditions to become transcendent.

Summary of Practices and Reflections in this dimension:

- Practising Nothingness   70

- Identification Questions   72

- Personal Operating System   75

- Love and Compassion   88

- Identifying a Cause Bigger Than You   90

- Conscious Control   93

- Conscious Surrender   95

- Present Moment Awareness   102

Chapter 4

The Fourth Dimension: Aligning

The Shift to Third Level

The desire to make the shift to Third Level comes about through push and pull. There's the pull of the promise of a life beyond that in which we presently operate and there's the push of discontent; the nagging feeling that where we currently are is simply not satisfactory any longer. Many leaders feel just ground down by the present. They are leading worn out, stressed and demotivated staff, going through the daily routine of commute, meeting, e-mails and so on. This creates inner tension brought about by discontent with the present, and a future seemingly devoid of realistic hope but which retains a glimmer of longing for something better.

This imaginary future comes about through the constant churning of thought. In our undeveloped, conditioned state, one thought chases another as long as we are conscious beings. We identify with being 'this', then we identify with being 'that'. We worry, we plan, we feel imaginary pain. All of this is mixed up with the fleeting moments of being present as a leader at Levels One and Two. It is an entirely unenlightened and unsatisfactory place to be.

When we make the decision to shift to Level Three, we shatter the hard shell that surrounds us at the first two levels. In my coaching practice, I use an extremely powerful technique, known as Radical Release which is a process whereby we break free from the shackles of ego; we deal with discontent in the most powerful way possible by building up the frequency of the thing with which our ego is identified. When the frequency is maxed out, when it tips over the edge, when we get it as powerful as it can be, we break from it and rest back into stillness, into spaciousness. It is in this place where we often connect with Truth, a truth which lies beyond the vacillations of the mind.

I have a good friend, Joe Gagliano, who is a retired New York fire chief. He once said to me, "The answers aren't in the mind." "Richard", he said, "you have to recognise that the mind gives us a data stream of good and bad data. Often the bad data vastly outweighs the good data. Don't get me wrong, I don't hate my mind, but I don't trust it.".

How right he is. Without understanding the reality of the mind, you will never make the shift to Third Level. You have to move beyond the dissatisfaction brought about by identifying solely with the small mind and the ego and the churning of thought that it produces. But how to begin the shift? How to escape identification with that which we cannot trust?

Well, you have to of course start from where you are in the present moment. Start from the very place that you are in right now. With *you*. Do a self-audit. How are you with yourself? Are you happy to spend time alone? Do you like yourself? Do you love yourself? I would suggest that it is impossible to shift to Third Level without love for self. If you are not comfortable in your own skin, it will be mightily difficult to make the leap, to transcend what is normal and comfortable at First and

Second Levels. Therefore, try looking at yourself, at your body-mind-spirit system as if from the outside. See these parts of yourself and the whole of yourself as a lover may see them. Look back at yourself with love and compassion and forgiveness. Turn the arrow of love inwards. See the beauty and radiance and genius in yourself. You absolutely must see the broken and incomplete self as being perfect in its imperfection in order to move forwards. This is because the great leap to Level Three requires a dissolution of the old order. Level Three is radically different. It includes elements of the esoteric, opening to a whole new dimension of reality. Stay trapped in limited thought and limited self-love and the door to this new dimension will remain tight shut.

Paul, writing in Romans got this right when he said, *"Do not be conformed to this world, but be transformed by the renewal of your mind, that by testing you may discern what is the will of God, what is good and acceptable and perfect."* In my first book, Mind-Sprit Detox, I suggest a few affirmations which can help you to transform your thoughts and to cast of self-beliefs which are standing in your way. I list some of them here; you can use them as affirmations, or alternatively, try writing them down on card or sticky notes and use them as a key to contemplation:

- Today I commit to the renewal of my mind.
- Today my mind turns only to what is good.
- Today I submit to the transformational power of Spirit.
- Today I fill my thoughts only with what serves my highest purpose.
- Today I consciously discern healthy thought and discard unhealthy thought.

- Today I forgive deeply.
- Today I feel peace, love and joy.
- Today I renew my heart with the power of Truth.
- Today Christ Consciousness expands to fill my every thought, word and deed.
- Today Spirit guides my thoughts which powerfully manifest as action in the world around me.

As you shift your focus away from the mind and towards spirit, you will be able to gain a clearer sense of seeing. As with my friend, Joe, you will begin to recognise that you cannot trust your mind. You will also begin to see that you cannot run on the energy produced by the mind at Third Level. No – the shock of transcendence powerfully shifts you into another dimension. Mind energy is replaced by spiritual energy. Spiritual energy is of an entirely different order to that of mind energy. Negativity, lack and the mechanics of operational management are replaced by abundance, limitless possibility and the wide open vistas of the seemingly impossible coming into form.

I like to use the analogy of the jet stream to understand this. The jet stream is a fast flowing, meandering air current that flows from West to East in the northern/polar region and the opposite way around in the Southern Hemisphere. This is no ordinary wind – it's an air current that can move at well over 200 mph. When commercial flights fly from West to East, they can fly into the jet stream and it becomes a free ride – a bit like a moving walkway at the airport. You walk at a normal pace, but get propelled forwards at impressive velocity, with very little effort on your own part. In February 2020, a British Airways 747, which normally flies at around 560 mph hit an incredible ground speed of 825 mph when it used the jet stream to help it on its way. It completed the flight from New York JFK to London Heathrow in a mere 4 hours and 56 minutes.

In the same way, we can use a power greater than ourselves - spirit - always available, always with us, around us and in us, to propel us forward with supernatural speed and perfect timing. Real power comes not from our small selves, but from a force much, much greater than us. Key to achieving take off, firstly of getting up to cruising altitude and secondly to get yourself into the powerful winds of the jet stream, is to understand that where power resides.

A fundamental mistake made by many new managers is to think that they need to get a grip, to rule with a heavy hand and to cover up any self-deficiencies by looking powerful. An obvious rookie mistake is to pretend that we're someone that we are not; to play the part of the great imagined leader, to project power over others. This route is always bound towards failure. Such leaders will always be uncovered for the fraud that they are; nobody wants to follow somebody lacking in authenticity or hungry for first-person power.

Power is actually a very interesting phenomenon in leadership. I once did a two year course run out of the UK Cabinet Office, called the 'Public Leadership Scheme'. It was designed by the then Prime Minister, Tony Blair, and it was borne of his frustration that there didn't seem to be enough high quality leadership in the civil service or in government agencies. There were about a hundred of us, half from the civil service, the remainder from GCHQ (the government's intelligence and security operation); the army; the police; the health service; highways and transport.

One evening session after dinner, we had a talk by the head of the British Civil Service. He said that his main interest in the role was around the subject of power: what it was, who had it, how to increase your power, how to lose it and so on. This distinguished post holder headed up the civil service under Margaret Thatcher, one of the most influential, bombastic and charismatic leaders the UK has ever seen. What staggered our speaker, however, was that even Mrs Thatcher constantly complained that she had no power! She would frequently rant about not being able to get anything done because power resided elsewhere – with ministers, with civil servants, with heads of quangos and so on. And when he questioned all of the latter people how they felt, they all would make the same complaint - that they all also lacked any real power.

His conclusion from all of this? That there is indeed power somewhere but that nobody thinks that they have much. The only possible conclusion, especially if somebody as powerful as Margaret Thatcher thought that she had no power, was that everybody actually has more power than they give themselves credit for. This is a lesson that I have never forgotten. I have since always looked for the ripples of influence that I might have that I otherwise might not notice. I have also tried to assume that I have more power and influence than my small ego might let me think. As with so much else, it becomes a self-fulfilling prophecy.

In reaching for transcendence, however, it's important that we look a little deeper – we need to transcend our initial ego-based understanding of what power actually is. So as a leader, ask yourself the question, 'what you are a conduit of?' If power is an energy, where does this power come from? Where does it reside?

At First Level, i.e. transactional leadership, we may either not be aware of power, or we might be desperate to project it inappropriately given lack of authenticity, lack of self-confidence, or lack of experience.

At Second Level, i.e. transformational leadership, power might be exercised with a degree more control and direction (see Conscious Control – see chapter 7).

At Third Level, i.e. Transcendent Leadership, our entire relationship with the very notion of power is shifted dramatically. Here we begin to recognise that it is not our human power that achieves greatness, but it is the power and magnificence of the universe manifesting through our team that ultimately powers our mission.

> "Power isn't control at all - power is strength, and giving that strength to others. A leader isn't someone who forces others to make him stronger; a leader is someone willing to give his strength to others that they may have the strength to stand on their own."
>
> *Beth Revis, Across The Universe*

To fully unleash power that transcends our small minds and imaginations, we have to lose all notions of human earthly power. It is in this space that we become one with the authentic self. When we lose pretensions of power, of ego, of self-centred ambition, and we shift towards our translucent self, and are driven by an ambition for the goal of the team, then we open to universal flow. We also experience the shift from hierarchical power to distributed power, the power that comes from within the team. As in the words of Dwight Eisenhower: "Leadership is the art of getting someone else to do something you want done because (s)he wants to do it."

When we finally emerge into the place where we come into alignment with our true genius and our highest good, then we begin to recognise that the work that we are doing in a leadership capacity is not our own work. We recognise that it is the work of Spirit, of divine love.

We and our team are merely the conduit through which the universe moves and functions. Our human self, small as it is, does not contain the power. Sure, we have some power but it is ultimately limited. Open up to the divine, transcend the small, 'I', and you open yourself up not as a receptacle of power but as a channel for power, power which is entirely different in nature to that of the struggling egotist that you might see at Levels One and Two.

> "The more conscious we become, the more powerful we become. We don't necessarily become miracle workers, but as we begin to awaken and our state of consciousness opens, different capabilities within us come online and are available to us."
>
> Adyashanti, Resurrecting Jesus

The journey from my head to my heart was a long and at times painful one. I studied economics for many years, starting at age 14 and going through to degree and masters level. I was Head of Planning and Performance for a large mental health organisation in London. On the 'Belbin' team roles model, I came out as a monitor-evaluator. I was strongly left brained and very analytical-thought oriented. I had deep suspicion of acting on instinct or of using the right-brain too much. Or so I thought. I worked directly to the Chief Executive, Stephen Firn, in the latter organisation and he used to constantly tell me what a big right brain I had, but I just couldn't see it. With the benefit of hindsight, maybe he was predicting the potential rather than the present-day actual, or perhaps he was seeing something I myself couldn't or didn't want to see.

Anyhow, in beginning to study more esoteric and advanced practice under people like Arjuna Ardagh, Deepak Chopra and Todd Jason, my consciousness was piqued and little by little, I began to see the advantages in exploring the power of intuition; of making a conscious shift from the head down to the heart centre. What really pushed me was when my good friend Remko, a Dutch ex-IBM executive, and I were asked to accompany Arjuna Ardagh to teach at the No Mind Festival in Sweden (the Angsbacka festival, made famous by the movie, 'Three Miles North of Molkom'). Sitting in our tent one balmy evening, Remko said to me, 'Richard – you really need to get out of your head and start to use your heart more'.

Now, I really needed that. It was one of the most important things that anybody has ever said to me. But it was still quite a shock and rather painful at the time to hear it. I was evermore conscious that I had to do this. Indeed, my friend Rev. Paul John Roach once told me, 'the journey from head to heart is one of the longest you will ever make'. I had a very powerful instinctive draw towards the truth of what Remko had told me. Since that time, I haven't stopped using my left brain. Indeed, my colleagues recently bought me a mug that says, 'I love spreadsheets!' emblazoned across it. But like I said earlier, it's a both/and universe. We can expand the right brain at absolutely no cost to the left.

When operating at Second Level, a brilliant technique that the Chief Executive I mentioned above, Stephen Firn, taught me, was the notion of tight-loose. You default to loose, i.e. give people and teams space, empowerment and the tools to operate. However, when the occasion dictates, you need sometimes to go 'tight', i.e. monitor rigorously; supervise closely. Knowing when to go tight and when to go loose is a vital skill. I probably only go really tight on something or somebody three or four times a year. Typically it will be if there's somebody in the wider team who isn't performing, or if there is a process or project that needs a great deal of monitoring or attention at a granular level.

At Third Level, we move beyond this. It doesn't mean that we reject the useful tools and techniques that we learn at Second Level. I still use tight/loose as well as a myriad of other traditional management tools. However, when we shift to Level Three, it just means that we transcend this plane, i.e. we move through and beyond the tools that we learn at First and Second Levels. I'd suggest that you consider now for a moment or two the activities that you lead and then draw up a list of them against 'tight-loose' criteria. Feel into each activity or function and whether they should best be managed in either a tight or a loose fashion. It's maybe the case that some functions belong in the opposite category to that which you're currently using.

****

The more we shift from head to heart, the more we come into alignment between all operating frequencies – the inner and the outer. It is then that we begin to see alignment and synchronicities all over the place. We might stumble across seeming coincidences, large and small, or sense coherent frequencies within our team and across departments.

The power of coherent frequencies cannot be overestimated. In the world of science, an example of this is given by William A. Tiller in his book, "Science and Human Transformation: Subtle Energies, Intentionality and Consciousness". He writes,

"The shift from incoherence to coherence can bring dramatic effects: a 60-watt light bulb whose light waves could be made coherent as a laser, would have the power to bore a hole through the sun - from 90 million miles away."

The coherent state described by Tiller can also be manifest in our lives when we connect with the state of unbounded mind, the state at which we shift beyond space-time, when we lift our vibration beyond the field of the small self and connect with Spirit. When we reach this stage, or rather, connect with that which is forever present, we come into coherence with all that is, the universal aspect of mind that both transcends and connects everything. From this place, creativity arises; things that had been held in mind become manifest; individuated consciousness begins to vibrate together in coherence. This is when we begin to observe synchronicities all around us. For this reason, coincidence is rarely an illusion. Coincidence is the outward form of coherence.

When we begin to practice at Level Three, we create the conditions for coherence at all levels and aspects of life, internal, external, individual and group. Coherence isn't just associated with and borne out of the shift from head to heart. I introduced Ken Wilber, the eminent spiritual philosopher and polymath, in the last chapter. Wilber speaks extensively in his writings about the notion of quadrants. Quadrants contain those elements I have just mentioned:
1) the inner life of individuals
2) the observable outer life of individuals
3) the inner life of collective peoples
4) the observable outer life of collective peoples

We have the tools to co-create coherence within all four quadrants in our practice at Level Three. The notion of quadrants is a brilliant foundational component of Wilber's seminal work, 'Integral Theory'. The building blocks of quadrants are 'holons'. Holons are something that are simultaneously a part and a whole, or an entity that can exist on it's own whilst also being a hierarchical part of a larger whole.

For example, a seed is in a tree and a tree is in a seed. A cell is both whole as a cell on its own, but it can also make up an organism. The organism is a collection of cells. An individual employee is in an organisation but the organisation is made up of individual employees plus capital and so on. Here is the definition of a holon in more detail:

"A holon is maintained by the throughput of matter-energy and information-entropy connected to other holons and is simultaneously a whole in itself and at the same time is nested within another holon and so is a part of something much larger than itself. Holons range in size from the smallest subatomic particles and strings, all the way up to the multiverse, comprising many universes.

Individual humans, their societies and their cultures are intermediate level holons, created by the interaction of forces working upon us both top-down and bottom-up. On a non-physical level, words, ideas, sounds, emotions - everything that can be identified - is simultaneously part of something, and can be viewed as having parts of its own…"

https://en.wikipedia.org/wiki/Holon_(philosophy)

As you move up the string of components, you encounter 'holarchies', whereby a whole is part of another whole, e.g. a word is part of a sentence which is part of a paragraph which is part of a chapter. Russian dolls are an obvious example of a holarchy.

Each holon can be seen to be a part of a quadrant, i.e. it can be seen to have a subjective, interior life, and an objective, exterior life. For example, the mind cannot be seen – it is interior and subjective. Your arm can be seen and felt. It is exterior and objective. Both the mind and the arm are part of *you*, but they inhabit different quadrants.

As well as things being able to be mapped into inner and outer expressions, there is a further dimension - things can also be seen from an individual and from a collective viewpoint.

Here's what the quadrants look like:

	INTERIOR	EXTERIOR
INDIVIDUAL	Individual Interior	Individual Exterior
COLLECTIVE	Collective Interior	Collective Exterior

Different professional disciplines tend to practice in particular quadrants to the exclusion of others. Let's consider some examples of which disciplines might reside within which quadrant. Firstly, take the interior individual, top left quadrant - the discipline of psychology resides in this space. It is concerned with the inner life of individual people.

However, when we look at the inner life of a group of people, we describe culture, so anthropologists and organisational development practitioners will be concerned with this quadrant, the collective interior world. This is the lower left quadrant.

The upper right quadrant is individual exterior, i.e. physically observable phenomena associated with individuals. General Practitioners, i.e. medics, will be interested in this. If you can poke it or chop it off, then that's the field of doctors, not psychologists!

The lower right quadrant is the field of functional or systematic theory when applied to the collective. This is the field inhabited by political theorists and economists.

Thus we can see that when we are describing the theory of Transcendent Leadership, we can locate different aspects of it in different quadrants. For example, if we're talking about conscious surrender, that's something that has to be worked on for each individual. It is an interior practice. It cannot be seen. It belongs to the upper left hand quadrant.

Different professional disciplines residing in and practising from singular quadrants presents the world with a considerable problem. For example, the medic might be faced with an individual who has diabetes triggered by obesity. The medic is trained to concentrate only upon the individual in front of them (top right quadrant). You never have whole groups of people turning up in the consulting room for a single appointment. However, the obesity might be a systemic issue within a family or a community. That's where the public health doctor comes in. But the public health doctor again is inhabiting only one quadrant (bottom right) to the exclusion of the others.

The problem this creates is that each of the quadrants ultimately describes a different view of the whole, hence why it is known as, 'Integral Theory'. Each quadrant therefore offers a complementary view of the whole rather than a competing view of reality. So as enlightened practitioners at Third Level, our instinct is absolutely not to fall into this trap of myopic practice.

How effective would a Transcendent Leader be if he or she only ever thought about their own inner world? Not effective at all of course! They need to be thinking about Third Level systems (bottom right quadrant); culture (bottom left quadrant); and behaviour (top right quadrant). I would challenge you when reading this book to have a think about different dimensions of Transcendent Leadership and map where in the quadrants each element resides.

Furthermore, when you are yourself developing your own practice, try to ensure wherever possible that the solution and intentions cover as many of the quadrants as possible. This will vastly improve the leverage and effectiveness of your approaches because they will reside in all aspects of 'what is'. For example, developing systems (bottom right) with no regard to how people feel about them (top left), how the culture of the organisation might receive those systems (bottom left) and how individuals operate those systems (top right) is a futile exercise, doomed to failure.

This is a key reason for the failure in attempting to introduce 'Toyota-esque' Lean Management techniques into the English Health system – it considered only the technical, systems issues (bottom right quadrant) with little regard as to how to embed within organisational cultures (bottom left quadrant) or obtain individual buy-in (top left quadrant).

The real key, then, is to achieve alignment across all quadrants. This ensures consistency of message and application. So the values that you hold dear as a leader in the upper left quadrant must align with the values of your team in the lower left. They need to be seen in your actions, top right and upheld by your systems, bottom right.

Let us shift our attention to the bottom left quadrant, the Interior Collective quadrant. This is where culture resides. As a Third Level Leader, you absolutely cannot ignore this quadrant. Once you have made the shift to transcendence, your task is essentially to engineer the shift in your team or organisation – to create a Third Level Organisation! To get from the individual (you) to the collective (the organisation/team), you will inevitably have to use Third Level techniques.

In my experience, by practising and embodying the shift in myself, the shift becomes manifest in all of those closest to me. This happens by a process of osmosis as well as teaching, coaching and mentoring of my line reports and other members of the team closest to me. It is such a powerful way of being that these people then also transmit the shift to those within their sphere of influence and beyond. The shift can then be rapid, and is explained by the 10 per cent rule and the 'Hundredth Monkey Effect.'

Let me first explain the 10 per cent rule. In 2011, Scientists at Rensselaer Polytechnic Institute in the US discovered that when just 10 per cent of the population holds an unshakable belief, their belief will always be adopted by the majority of the society:

"The scientists, who are members of the Social Cognitive Networks Academic Research Center (SCNARC) at Rensselaer, used computational and analytical methods to discover the tipping point where a minority belief becomes the majority opinion. The finding has implications for the study and influence of societal interactions ranging from the spread of innovations to the movement of political ideals.

When the number of committed opinion holders is below 10 percent, there is no visible progress in the spread of ideas. 'It would literally take the amount of time comparable to the age of the universe for this size group to reach the majority," said SCNARC Director Boleslaw Szymanski, the Claire and Roland Schmitt Distinguished Professor at Rensselaer. 'Once that number grows above 10 percent, the idea spreads like flame.'

As an example, the ongoing events in Tunisia and Egypt appear to exhibit a similar process, according to Szymanski. 'In those countries, dictators who were in power for decades were suddenly overthrown in just a few weeks.'"

Source: https://news.rpi.edu/luwakkey/2902

This has also often been popularised as the 'Hundredth Monkey Effect'. The story of the hundredth monkey effect was published in Lyall Watson's foreword to Lawrence Blair's Rhythms of Vision in 1975. The story involves scientists who were conducting a study of macaque monkeys on the island of Kōjima in 1952. These scientists noted that a group of the monkeys learned to wash sweet potatoes before eating them, and gradually this new behaviour spread throughout a younger generation of monkeys. This happened in the usual fashion, through observation and repetition.

The breakthrough in understanding, however, was that the researchers observed that once a critical number of monkeys was reached, that is, the hundredth monkey, this previously learned behaviour instantly spread across the water to monkeys on nearby islands.

I will not expatiate further on the world of 'quadrant engineering' and organisational development as this belongs mainly in the world of Second Level. However, knowing how to identify and understand quadrants and then being able to reconcile them and create meaning, connection and coherence across quadrants, is a foundational skill for the Transcendent Leader. It would be short-sighted of the enlightened leader to think that he or she could reach transcendence if they were only operating within one of the quadrants. Transcendence is, by its very nature, holistic, therefore all quadrants within the holarchy need to be integrated into the whole of transcendent practice.

How we go about doing this is vital. We could easily get drawn down the rabbit hole of complexity at this point. Organisational development is nothing if not complex. Is it possible instead to strip away and simplify in our attempt to incorporate Wilber's Integral Theory within the practice of Transcendent Leadership? How do we go about aligning all of the elements of our leadership practice across all quadrants? I would argue that it is best done with simplicity.

I love simplicity. Our minds are so vast that they tend to be addicted to complexity. We must resist – complexity of approach in leadership rarely serves us well. As such, a book that I have drawn great inspiration from is, 'Simple Rules: How to Thrive in a Complex World' by Kathy Eisenhardt and Donald Sull. This type of literature stands at the cusp of Second and Third Level understanding. It's not necessarily entirely within the world of the transcendent but it is most definitely pointing that way, a gateway to the transcendent as it were. This is because it begins the shift into a new, less complex, less mechanistic way of reimagining the organisation and your place in it as a leader. It is more than merely transformational because if you get it right, it will create space for the transcendent, for the preternatural, to take place.

Let me tell you about how I have used its concepts and its solutions of simplicity in my team. Firstly the simple rules: Eisenhardt and Sull ask, 'what's the point of having a strategy if barely anybody in the organisation knows what it is?' Furthermore, if you indeed think that it is useful for everybody to indeed know what the strategy is, it has to be simple. If the strategy is a massive tome that covers all the angles, is beautifully written, and runs into thousands of words, then it will remain on the shelf in the CEO's office and it will never be read. On the other hand, a few beautifully crafted rules can transform large and complex organisations, organisations that often span the globe. This in turn allows for faster, better decision making.

When I first encountered this notion, I was very much drawn to it. I therefore started thinking hard, using my left brain, as to what the rules could be for my own team. Try as I might, however, I couldn't figure it out. I was using the wrong part of my brain at the wrong frequency and at the wrong level, i.e. Level Two. It took me a fortnight to become conscious of my error. When I recognised my mistake, I shifted into Level Three, and asked the universe for a download.

A 'download' is what I call a packet of incoming information that comes from a place outside of myself, i.e. it is exogenous. I turn to downloads when I have come to a dead end, when I have found myself unable to find an answer or resolve a situation using my own mental and cognitive faculties (i.e. using techniques at Levels One and Two). As with all Level Three techniques, it is remarkably simple. You formulate a question and imagine throwing it up into the sky above your head. You let it go – you put it out there into the field. In so doing, you are opening a direct line to source; you are humbling yourself by getting out of the way and admitting that you yourself have no answer.

On this occasion, two weeks later, when I wasn't expecting it (I was actually mowing the lawn, which, along with driving and taking a shower, I find one of the most receptive activities for downloads), the download came to me. All three rules burst into my consciousness at once, BANG! It was quite a revelation to me.

Downloads always come in a flash. They originate not from your mind, but from 'Big Mind', the Universe, therefore, they will never feel as if they come from your own imagination or from thought. You will absolutely know and feel that they come from outside of you. Furthermore, because they come from Source, they carry a very high frequency, hence their arriving as a single packet of information, however lengthy they may be. This high frequency not only means that the information arrives suddenly, but it also prompts you to act quickly. There is a sense of urgency about a download.

Anyhow, on this occasion, a single packet of high frequency information came to me in a single rapid flash. I then sat down and unwrapped the information, and in so doing discovered the three rules which were as follows:

1) Be the person [fully empathise with the person you're treating, see the world through their eyes, using a strength (asset) based approach].
2) Be the service [you are the service and the service is *you*; as with each of the seven trillion cells in our body - the DNA of the entire bodily system is contained within each of the cells; the body is therefore holarchic in nature].
3) Be happy [be joyful and satisfied in your work; be the professional you always dreamt of being; give off good vibes to patients and colleagues and the placebo effect will be given full reign in both healing people and motivating co-workers].

And that's it. Three rules – be the person, be the service, be happy. A mere eight words that have guided all team operations and philosophy in my own practice for five years now; five years in which we have gone from being good to being off-the-scale great! It's that simple.

So what exactly happened here? Well, I took a concept that sits on the cusp of Second and Third Level. By receiving the rules through an intensely Third Level practice (downloading) and applying them within a Third Level environment, the rules took on Third Level qualities. Once set in motion, I saw them moving amongst people and almost taking on a life of their own. Try it for yourself. Ask the universe to give you a download of three or four simple rules for your team or organisation. It could revolutionise your practice.

In the current year to date, my team has embedded no fewer than fifty achievements, all of which have had a positive impact on the lives of patients across our district, and some of which have been absolutely ground-breaking, and which have never previously been implemented (or indeed even thought of) elsewhere in the county. When we sat down to compile this list, we were absolutely blown away by the extent of the achievements. We didn't set out to do so much; indeed, whilst we work hard, none of us had worked particularly long hours (with the odd exception when need dictated) and all of us were in great health mentally and physically. In other words, the quality of the rules being implemented within Third Level has created an environment within which enormous amounts can be achieved with minimum effort. Proof to me that we had hit cruising altitude.

Through practising simplicity, understanding quadrants, appropriately applying tight-lose and so on, we are able to fulfil the imperative within Integral Theory, that we need to wake up and to grow up. We wake up to the reality of what we're dealing with, i.e., the world is too complex to control solely using Newtonian mechanistic forms of control, such as comprehensively applying Standard Operating Procedures (SOPs).

SOPs are often used too liberally in organisations, particularly in bureaucracies where everything employees do has to conform to a policy directive, which ends up sucking the life and creativity out of the organisation. *(Note, we still have a need for SOPs and policies – don't forget that Level Three is built upon the foundations of Level Two and Level Two commensurately is built upon the foundations of Level One; each level is built upon and includes the previous level; it transcends, it doesn't destroy the previous level).*

We need also to *grow up*; to treat staff and colleagues as adults with brains capable of making complex decisions in a complex world. As such, we accept the responsibility that a greater degree of freedom will bring. Our least lofty ambition is to stop doing stupid things – we cast off the childish ways of Level One – slavish obedience to policy and transaction. Our most lofty ambition is one of brilliance: To fully realise the *brilliance* of all staff and teams thus to deliver a *brilliant* service to patients through a *brilliant* organisation. Thus a brilliant WHOLE.

I recall a time when one of our directors asked me how my team appeared to be delivering so much in such a laid back fashion. He said that everybody else was busting a gut and appearing on the ragged edge of stress and burn out, whereas my team appeared not to be making much of a physical and emotional effort, but seemed to be enjoying life and thriving as professionals. My reply? Much in line with the above; 'Brian, it's quite simple. You recruit brilliant people. You raise the consciousness of not so brilliant people or persuade them to leave. You then create a space within which brilliant people can be brilliant. You then sit back and watch the brilliance happen!'.

As with the hundredth monkey, when there's a movement of enough transcendent people in your team, your team as a whole will take on a new identity, the identity of brilliance that emerges through Third Level. And it doesn't stop there. It will then spread to other key leaders in the organisation. Eventually, this opens the possibility that the organisation itself will wake up and grow up, make the shift and transcend into a different plane and a new body corporate will arise. Hence a whole-scale alignment and transformation that is holarchic in nature, i.e. Third Level transformation that transcends the individual, team and organisation.

We can now summarise the fourth dimension of Transcendent Leadership: The shift to Third Level leadership occurs when you align head and heart and allow your awakened state to take control of the mind, thus creating coherence within and between yourself and the organisational body.

****

We have come now to the end of the foundational dimensions that unlock your transcendent journey to Level Three leadership. The final half of the book, the last four dimensions, are cyclical in nature – connecting, creating, doing and resting.

Summary of Practices and Reflections in this dimension:

- Self-Audit   105

- Tight-Loose   113

- Quadrant Mapping   119

- Simple Rules   123

- Downloads   124

Chapter 5

The Fifth Dimension: Connecting

The Centrality of Love

'Transcendence' means 'to jump beyond this current state'. It is a place where we create beautiful environments for people to thrive – for everyone, be them leaders, employees, customers, clients, passengers or patients. This is a living environment, thriving because of flow. And where there is flow, there is love. Love is the very substance that enables and carries flow because it is wrapped up in the ground of being from which all things arise. If you find yourself in a transcendent environment, you will know about it. It's visceral, the sense of love-born flow is palpable.

A few years ago, my organisation had been taken over by another public body. One of the directors had been touring our directorates and mine was the last one she and her entourage visited, probably given that we were furthest away from the new headquarters. After spending a couple of hours with my team, the director offered up this thought, 'Richard', she said, 'there's something remarkable about this team. It just feels so different to everywhere else that we have been. If we could bottle what we feel here and spread what you have everywhere else, I think everything would just fall into place'. She felt the flow.

Unfortunately, as this director was perhaps alluding to, the flow state is far from common. The reason that flow can be blocked is because 'love thy neighbour as thyself' doesn't always work. Love isn't flowing. The key reason is that we do not always love ourselves, in fact all too often, we hate ourselves. Maybe as a result, we don't cut off our own foot, rather, we metaphorically cut off our neighbour's foot or covet their possessions, or generally feel the scarcity. In the work situation, people do likewise – they do not share knowledge and learning; people cut others down in order to make themselves look taller; jealousies and gossip abound. The driving force is 'lack'.

Conversely, the Transcendent Leader comes from abundance. The Transcendent Leader refuses to come from scarcity or from fear, because they have learnt to move beyond that state. The Transcendent Leader experiences both an internal as well as an external unity of being. That is, they love both themselves and all around in equal measure, because the barriers between self and the world collapse as ego collapses.

Being aware, being awake and coming from the heart of love is what connects and binds the Third Level leader with the people around them. Think of the diversity of character, of behaviour, of personal and professional background within your team. It is now absolutely possible for your team to become a truly united force in your organisation, and in the world. When you, and your team, become anchored into something deeper, the connection becomes profound. The point of commonality, of singularity, which creates this connection, is enfolded within each of us.

The foundational dimensions of Transcendent Leadership lay the groundwork for us to become awake, conscious beings that are aware of being aware. We become like an ant walking around the surface of a doughnut – the toroidal nature of the doughnut ensures that every point on the surface is connected to every other point. There is only one surface. In the same way, awareness is folded back in on itself, hence the singularity, the oneness. Everywhere we go, everything we do becomes part of the whole. We can even go beyond the sense of connectedness to say that it is one thing. Every part of the surface of a toroid isn't merely connected to every other part. It's effectively all the same part!

It's not simply that we are conscious *of* something external to ourselves; we have the means to be awake to the consciousness itself. From this well of awakeness, a shared consciousness from within the team, everything comes forth – all creativity, all manifestation. Once we are anchored into this shared state of consciousness, then the singularity born of unity creates a coherent field from which is created truly radical, disruptive product, technology and service.

Eleanor Roosevelt once said, "To handle yourself, use your head; to handle others, use your heart." To master leadership is really to master life itself. When we transcend the ego, we experience a little death, the death of the 'small self'. We are then left with a heart of compassion which places love and giving firmly in the centre of our leadership practice. We experience a heartfelt intimacy with those around us because there is now no hierarchy of ego; there is a unity of consciousness that connects us with those that we lead at a level that can only be imagined at egoic levels of awareness.

The transcendence of ego brings about consciousness of universal unity. The folly of the false belief in two worlds – spirit and the material world – dissolves in the face of true awareness. The false concept of duality serves only the ego. When ego is transcended, the duality collapses.

In operating from awareness rather than from within the 'small self', the Transcendent Leader recognises his or her trigger points and helps their team look at *their* triggers. From the heart of love, when we see other people struggling, it is through eyes of empathy rather than judgement. And in those times when people attack us, and we would feel that we should fight back, our higher nature recognises that they are caught in struggle. The environment within which leaders operate is often a messy one, fraught with negativity, power struggles, ego and hierarchy. Now we have the tools to transcend that environment, and the fuel, the driver for every tool we have is love.

I would invite you at this point to spend some time in quiet reflection. Think about somebody with whom you sense a contraction, a frisson of negative reaction towards. Now feel into the struggles that they themselves might be having at this time. See through their eyes with compassion. Really feel into it from a heart of love. Now return to what it was about them that triggered you in the first place. Do you feel a dissipation of that contraction? How might you interact with them from this place hereon in?

I spoke in Chapter One of revelation, motivation and leverage. When you find yourself surrounded by the trials and tribulations that will surely come your way, just return to love. Return to the centrality of your divine being. Who or what are you (revelation)? What are you doing on the planet (motivation)? What tools do you have at your disposal (leverage)? When tough times or situations face you, there is simply no other way for the Transcendent Leader to face them apart from the heart of love, from a place of divine knowledge. Why not reflect on this now – write your own personal list of revelation, motivation and leverage. What is it telling you?

Just consider this compass question for a moment: what might your life look like if you fully embodied the spirit of love pouring itself into this world? Imagine with every out-breath, you send a wave of blessing upon which the spirit of love dances out in the manifest realm? Instead of maintaining a faint flickering of love and compassion within yourself, you open the window of the heart and let the abundance of divine love simply flood out into the world. Just contemplate how transformative that would be to you, the people you love and the world around you.

When we as leaders look around us at the environment within which we are operating, we often think to ourselves that there could not be a more oppressive, difficult place within which to lead and manage a team. How can we possibly display the higher qualities of leadership with this warfare taking place all around us? It is so easy to forget the lessons and revelation at this point, so easy to hit the rocks when these storms swirl around us.

But here it is, the answer is simple, profound and powerful beyond measure. The answer is love! There is no higher state of being, no higher vibration, no higher calling, no higher power. And if we are to reach for the stars and make the breakthrough into Level Three leadership, we simply have to fully embrace love in our practice. Indeed, it's not a case of calling on love, of incorporating it, or of using a bit of it. If we approach it in this way, maybe doing a bit more 'active listening', protecting supervision or one-to-one time, or feigning concern and empathy, then all we will be doing will be practising Level Two leadership. These are referred to as 'leadership behaviours' in Level Two leadership training. But behaviours are simply a manifestation of what is in your heart and in your head. They are a second order issue.

Over and over I have seen people trying from their own strength to modify unhelpful behaviours. The longest I ever give anybody when they are struggling to do this is three months. Then they revert back to previous behaviour patterns. This is because it's literally impossible to modify behaviour without fundamentally changing what sits behind the behaviour. It is simply too difficult, too much of a struggle. Therefore it can never last because it does not come from the authentic heart-centre. It comes from a place of scarcity.

The only way out of this trap is to connect with the authentic heart of true self. Discard any ambition of the ego and let yourself, your life, your being be the example:

> "If you would convince a man that he does wrong, do right. But do not care to convince him. Men will believe what they see. Let them see."

Henry David Thoreau

In order to practice love and thereby modify behaviour, you cannot simply use it as another management technique. It's not one of the tools in our management toolkit. To see it as this would be a simple exercise in reductionism. It would be an attempt to diminish the greatest power there is. Indeed, love is not something that you can incorporate or use. You have to actually *be* love. This love is not a thing that we obtain or that we can look for to bring into our practice. You first have to recognise that love comes from *within*, not without. It is *in* you. You *are* love. When you recognise and remove the blockages to the flow of love, it will rush out from you, it will emerge through every fibre of your being. We need to just tune into it. If you struggle with this, I would invite you to go to the meditations section of my web-site and do The Heart Meditation: https://www.awakeningcoaching.co.uk/meditations

It is a beautiful little practice and it enables us to connect with the truth of 'what is' within ourselves and to connect that with the outer world of form through the window of the heart. Do this every day for a week and see how it changes you.

When we do this and love flows, then the environment that we operate in will begin healing as love radiates. People will feel loved. When we tune in and share, we will recognise that it feels better to give than to receive. It feels incredible to give love without condition, without having any rules to love, without drawing any lines to love: love without delineation.

If we don't love ourselves fully and have a unity within ourselves, however, we create an impediment to the flow of love. When we let go of self-loathing or ego and slide into the reality of our truth, when we surrender and let go of the egoic self, we are able to incorporate and embody our humanity along with our divinity. The humanity and the divinity merge. This means that we can reconcile our experience of human emotions such as anger and loss and tiredness and frustration and still be in our divinity. We then become compassionate witnesses to our human experiences. We can observe and hold and cradle the feelings as if they were a child.

Divine surrender allows us to let go of everything that we think will bring us what we want – we let ambition and greed go in order to let what divinity has for us come in. When we connect with ourselves and with the divine, the new foundation of our life becomes divine embodiment.

We then experience oneness in ourselves – we circle back to experience our humanity as well as our divinity. Mind, body, spirit are simply manifestations of the same thing. Divinity is the source for all. There is no separateness, no division. We then extend that out to experience a more sustainable realisation of oneness with everyone, altogether, at one time. That is your team, your organisation, your family, the natural world, the planet, the cosmos. But to be able to experience this oneness, this connection with all, this love and compassion for all, we first need to be able to experience it within ourselves.

Thus it all starts and ends *within* us. If there is conflict and division within, then it is impossible to experience oneness *without*. If the prism that witnesses from our own consciousness is faulty, then it will be unable to reconcile the oneness without.

What is the nature of this love and compassion? How does it manifest within the organisational context? Let me stress that it isn't just all fluffy-bunny and mushy. Sometimes it's tough love – sometimes it's grabbing someone before they jump off a cliff. So love and leadership, love in business – it's not 'what you know and who you know', it's 'who you know and how much love abounds'. This love will obviously manifest in a completely different way to the love that you might have for your spouse or for your children. But it is no less powerful. People will see it in your eyes, feel it in your actions and in your motivations.

You will find that when you give the energy of love, that love comes back to you. It is transformative to your team beyond measure. Connection and the centrality of love is the first of the cyclical dimensions of leadership, as everything resides in love and is born from love and nothing else comes close to it. It's cyclical in nature because it has to be nurtured. It's no good laying down a foundation of love and then just letting it be. Just because I loved my children fully and unconditionally yesterday doesn't mean that love will flow today as well. I could be as ratty as hell today. Love is something that is practised in the moment.

That's another reason why love is absolutely fundamental to Third Level leadership. Love is something that cannot be stored up like the charge in a battery. It's something that is given and received in the 'now'. Love is the very building block, the matter upon which and through which consciousness and divine creation flows. Without such present awareness and creativity, Third Level leadership withers and dies.

There is probably nothing more important on this planet at this time than love and connection. The culture wars that are raging presently across the Western world manifest isolation and division and schism. Love brings unity, wholeness and peace. So there can be nothing more important to you in your walk on this earth as a leader at this time – you are not just bringing creativity and passion to your team, you're bringing it to the planet. You can learn all the techniques in the world, but without love and connection, they are utterly worthless. There is a Bible passage just screaming out to be quoted here, and I cannot resist. It says this better than I could ever hope to:

> "If I speak in the tongues of men or of angels, but do not have love, I am only a resounding gong or a clanging cymbal. [2] If I have the gift of prophecy and can fathom all mysteries and all knowledge, and if I have a faith that can move mountains, but do not have love, I am nothing. [3] If I give all I possess to the poor and give over my body to hardship that I may boast, but do not have love, I gain nothing."
>
> 1 Corinthians 13 v 1-3 NIV

When we step into our divinity, we step into the heart of love. The power and the resources are already within us. We do not need to look outside of ourselves. When we take this step into the divine, into love, we become the expression of God manifesting love and action in the things that we do and the people that we lead.

To experience transcendence in our leadership practice then, is to step into the magnificent heart of God. As the great theologian, Eric Butterworth once said, love doesn't come from God. Love *is* God! When Eben

Alexander returned from his Near Death Experience ('Proof of Heaven'), people asked him what he had learned. He said that it was very simple - if you want it in just one word, our mission, our purpose on this earth is to be a channel for love. If you want two words, you can add 'compassion' to that. And at Third Level leadership, you will find your heart opening with incredible passion and compassion for the people in your organisation. Your sense of hierarchy, whilst still present, fades as the ego fades. Any sense of being above anybody else begins to dilute and you begin to feel a great oneness and intimacy with the people that you lead. A sense of completeness and unity pervades everything.

Indeed, as I write this, I have just returned from a hospital that I manage. I spent the afternoon there, really just floating around with no great aim, apart from making heartfelt contact with the people in my team, letting flow take me where I had to be and to meet whomever I had to meet. I had a few wonderful encounters with people that felt like I was having exactly the right conversation with the right people at the right time. The last person I met was a nurse sat in an office speaking by 'phone to some rather contumacious relatives. I spent nearly an hour with her; she is in a crucial role on the ward, one that demands resilience, tact, diplomacy, perseverance and a high degree of nursing experience.

I can't tell you that any specific objectives were met during our time together (the stuff of First Level Leadership), but I can tell you that something powerful shifted in our meeting. There were all of the things outlined above – intimacy, joviality, a vision of what she was doing that was raised above the mundane transactional level. There was an energy in the room when I left that had been lacking from when I had arrived. Something had shifted. From an analysis of my left brain, I cannot tell you what that was. But in my heart, I knew that something wonderful and important had flowed between us that will have far reaching and positive implications for the team.

This is because there is another incredibly powerful aspect to connecting through love, and that is the ability at Third Level to be able to transmit energy. That is what I felt in this meeting. It has been happening with increasing frequency of late in my leadership practice. In addition to what happened today, I can recall several almost miraculous events that have taken place lately.

One such example was a recent coaching session I held with a manager in a neighbouring county. She had been struggling even to operate at Level One, let alone Three. I was on my third coaching session with her. I spent about an hour and a half with her recently. I had points to follow up with her from the previous session; I asked her some powerful questions as you do as a coach.

But the key feature that transformed our session was that we entered what I call a 'flow transmission'. This is a beautiful and powerful experience for both parties. Essentially, I simply imagine myself (in terms of my gross consciousness, my thoughts, my ego), stepping aside and letting the power of the universe flow through me, down through my crown chakra, and out of the window of my heart and into the other person.

The feeling of transmission of something greater, much greater than me, is at the same time both invigorating and also strangely draining. This was happening for much of the session in fact, and the person whom I was coaching was almost growing before my eyes. It was as if a light had gone on inside her. Ideas and inspiration began to pepper her conversation in a way that they hadn't before. When she finally left the office, she said, 'wow, that was really quite something. I can't thank you enough. This is going to be an amazing week!'

This 'flow transmission' continued when I got home. I had a call from a colleague who was in two minds about applying for a job I had put out to advert. He sounded full of doubt and deflated. I knew that he had the potential to be a great leader if given the chance, so I wanted him to apply. Again, I was conscious throughout of connecting to him on a different level, a higher level, well, Third Level to be exact. I felt the power flowing once more and I felt him growing and shifting in outlook as the conversation progressed. We weren't even in the same town at the time, but it demonstrates the laws of non-local quantum mechanics in action. He finished the call sounding like a changed man – invigorated, confident and most definitely going to apply for the job.

> *"...But in 1935, Einstein and two younger colleagues unwittingly stumbled upon what looks like the strangest quantum property of all, by showing that, according to quantum mechanics, two particles can be placed in a state in which making an observation on one of them immediately affects the state of the other—even if they're allowed to travel light years apart before measuring one of them. Two such particles are said to be entangled, and this apparent*

> *instantaneous "action at a distance" is an example of quantum nonlocality."*

> *The Atlantic: How Quantum Mechanics Could Be Even Weirder June 22 2016, Philip Ball*

Why don't you give it a go? Try doing this practice: Know that your energy field does not begin and end where your body ends. You give out a life energy. The notion of what seems like solid matter such as a table or your body for that matter, being actually 'solid' is something of an illusion caused by our limitations of perception. Life is energy and therefore we and other people are way more sensitive to energy and energy flows than you might think.

You can have a little experiment with your energy. Don't make this obvious, but next time you're in a small meeting, be present, do what you have to do, but imagine yourself like a piece of cardboard for a while. Take in and give out no energy. Sense how the room is. Then switch the flow on; open the crown and the heart chakras; shift your 'small' self out of the way and let the energy fill the room. See what happens? Now try this again and again and again until it becomes habitual.

You may find yourself getting tired after this practice. Take it easy. Drink plenty of water.

The four compass questions we can ask around this are:

- Are we connecting or disconnecting?

- Are we coming from love or fear? (associated with this polarity is a wonderful question that I ask if I find myself getting too stuck in my mind when considering a problem – 'what would love do?')

- Are we coming from abundance or scarcity?

- When you feel the calling to step into this leadership role steered by the divine heart of love, how do you respond?

These four compass questions help to point the Transcendent Leader in the right direction. They are pointers that help us become more conscious of connecting from a heart of love. They help to promulgate flow and the transmission of energy.

Asking questions is a powerful intervention in Transcendent Leadership practice. When coaching, I try to avoid giving clients direct answers to their issues. Even when I am not in a formal coaching session, I like to remind myself to use coaching questions wherever possible. Obviously at times, as a leader, you go into 'tight' and directive mode, but the power of coaching is that rather than spoon-feed answers to people, as an adult might do to a child, you instead elicit the answer from the person to whom you are speaking. It is a non-hierarchical technique, maintaining adult to adult communication and it enables the person to reveal the answer for themselves.

The answer is always found within – and when a client or a colleague finds themselves searching for the answer, the questions produce a psycho-active response in the person's brain. It takes them on a transformative journey by working through options and solutions themselves.

As a leader, you tend to be the recipient of problems. Whenever people find themselves 'stuck', or they hit their limits of delegated authority or personal expertise, they fire problems up the line. The problems that people will come to you with typically fall into two camps:

1) Something that they have but don't want, e.g. anxiety; an overspent budget.

2) Something that they don't have but do want, e.g. a better paid job; a difficult employee.

It's worth sifting the problems that come your way into these two camps because it helps begin the questioning process. For instance, with the former, you can ask, 'what would you like to have happen?'; for the latter, 'then what happens?'.

You can then follow up with what is often referred to as 'clean language' (devised by David Grove in the 1980s). Clean language is a way of ensuring that you are not leading the other person with tendentious questions, hence they are 'clean' of any of your own prejudices and input. Here are some examples:

- Is there anything else about...

- What kind of...

- Whereabouts...

- Is there a relationship between...

- What needs to happen for...

- What do you need to do...

- Can you...

- Will you...

Again, once you have delivered a powerful question, it is important not to interrupt when the other person is processing. Given that these are powerful questions and not merely small talk, you will often find that it takes some time for an answer to be forthcoming. Stay with the silence because this is when the other person's neuro-network is developing. The psycho-active processing is what makes the solution pathways they devise so 'sticky', because the very structure of their brain is altering and developing through the process of internally working out the solution.

Shifting towards the adoption of more of a coaching style is central to the Transcendent Leader as it creates a powerful connection with the people in your team that is based upon love. That might sound a bit over the top and it is obviously not connected with romantic love, rather a deep and abiding affection for the people that you lead. If you cared not a jot for your team, it's frankly easier to give them the answer you have thought of and get them off the 'phone or out of your office as quickly as possible. But because you have love for your team and for the person, you take the time to use coaching questions. It transforms the person and it transforms the team. They will then more likely use coaching techniques with their own team and thus the neuro-network that is the team itself continues to learn and to flourish.

When I practised from Level Two understanding, I used to reach for questions if I found myself 'stuck'. It was a slightly cynical way to throw the ball back in the other person's court if I didn't know the answer to something myself. 'Quick, think of a question!', I'd say to myself. Now that I practise from the consciousness of Level Three, I come from a place of love, of connection and of authenticity and I use powerful questions and clean language as part of my day to day practice because I know how much growth comes from this.

There are so many tools and techniques in the leader's toolbox that can come from a place of cynicism. NLP is often used as a manipulative tool to connect with people. This just won't wash at Third Level. Coming from a place of genuine authenticity must form a part of everything that you think, say and do. It is bound to and lives within all that you are as a leader at Level Three. Transcendent Leadership requires the most authentic self to be present in all aspects of leadership. This is why the awareness of 'love' is so central to the whole notion of transcendence within leadership practice. Inherent and implicit within this is the connection between one soul and another.

I deliberately say, 'soul' rather than, 'person' or 'employee' or 'team member' because when you shift your understanding of that person away from just being another member of the body corporate, or somebody on a staff register, then you begin to see them as the whole person that they really are. When you see the person within, the person undivided from that which lives a life outside of the organisation, then you begin to create the conditions by which you can connect on a deeper level.

Whilst questions are the door through which creativity begins, the subsequent connection through coaching begins and ends with *listening*. Much has been said about the different levels of listening in management and coaching literature. They are often described as:

- Ignoring: not really listening at all.

- Pretend listening: you might seem like you're listening but in fact, you are distracted or you might be doing something else entirely, such as looking at your computer or your 'phone.

- Selective Listening: you are zoning in and out of paying attention to the speaker.

- Attentive Listening: you are listening but rather than really connecting, your mind is thinking about when it can jump in, or what response to make.

- Empathic Listening: You attempt to get into the head of the person speaking; connect with them; see the world through their eyes.

- Generative Listening: Your connection with the other person generates and gives birth to something new.

In transcendence, however, almost none of those levels suffice. Even empathetic listening is often little more than attentive listening done well. This is because the listening is still centred on the notion of separation. You listen; the other person speaks. Two people making some kind of a connection.

I prefer to shift focus much more deeply into something described by Otto Scharmer of Massachusetts Institute of Technology (MIT) which he calls, 'Dynamic Presencing'. This is where you, the listener, come from the heart – you deepen your presence with the other person and open the window of the heart to the other person. Again, the Heart Meditation is a beautiful way to bring this practice to life.

True presence is achieved when you understand and get into tune with the heart meditation, practice asking powerful questions to the person that you are with and deepen your reflective listening with an open heart. I would challenge you to try this for yourself. Feel into what the other person is saying with the window of your heart fully open. Rest in the spaciousness of what the other person is saying; recognise the heart as a jewel. You will find that great clarity results as the boundary between you and the other person begins to dissolve.

Dynamic Presencing is co-creative. As the experience of the exchange begins to bring the two of you closer together, use your own energy and intuition to clear away the debris for the other person; present possibilities rather than advice; let the other person uncover their own truth. Come to the conversation with Absolute Certainty that the other person has all the answers within them already; your task of discovery is to uncover and give birth to the solutions.

Continue to bring the conversation back to what is real in the moment. Know that the past exists only as a thought. The past is not really here. You don't have to ask the other person to drop it, but you gently guide them to stop seeing thoughts as a reality. Guide them to seeing what is real and present right in this moment. The past is not current and in the moment it can exist only as a thought. Hence the past nearly always becomes an encumbrance to the discovery of what is real, as what is real has to exist in the present moment. It cannot exist in any other moment.

Furthermore and very importantly, in your heart-based communication, give the other person the permission to *feel*. Acknowledging feelings is one of the hardest things to bring into the corporate space. People have been conditioned over years to see feelings as something not to be trusted; something illogical; something that is taboo in the organisational context. Yet feelings are the very essence of the transcendent. Feelings and intuition are central to Dynamic Presencing. Furthermore, when you are in this space, be comfortable with it. Whatever arises is right to arise.

Hold the heart-centred space; don't step in there with advice – change your old habit and don't be pulled inwards to solve problems. You can use your own words and experience to re-frame and clarify what the other person is saying – that's OK, but don't stand in the way of their fullest expression in the moment.

I hope that it is becoming clear just how far away the Transcendent Leader is from any Second Level notion of listening because Transcendent Leadership is not just a set of techniques – it is a way of being – it is disruptive technology applied to and residing in the heart! This is because there is a real distinction between empathy and rapport. As I briefly mentioned above, many trainers suggest the use of Neuro Linguistic Programming (NLP), which at its basic level can be as simple as behavioural mimicking. This is absolutely not in the territory of Third Level! We are working with integrity through the heart meditation which drops you into the vibration where you are breathing the other person's feelings into your own; you will experience the other person's excitement and pain and joy as your own. There is no separation, and it is not a potentially manipulative or cynical method as NLP can be when not used from a place of authenticity.

Through this listening practice, you will experience a devolution and emancipation of power. Power is no longer held at the top. It is not a monopoly that belongs to you, the leader. When you create this presencing, you hold the space for the other person to flourish and develop. A beautiful energy is created and charged and the movement of that energy is directed by spirit. When you discover this space, you will not see it as a technique or as an accomplishment. You will simply relax into a very beautiful space, a space within which creativity can burst forth and resolutions emerge. The listening process therefore becomes an experience, something that you sink into with all of you – your ears, your mind, your body and your higher awareness attuned to subtle energies. That is truly transcendent in its nature.

****

A note of caution at this point. As you continue to transcend, and as you grow in your knowledge and practice in Third Level, you will invariably encounter opposition. In being a beacon of light, you will carry with you and transmit numinous qualities that awake jealousy and opposing energies in some souls; you may light the shadows that do not want to be lit. The road can get bumpy at times as artefacts of other people's egos become obstacles on your journey.

An example of this in my life was in using Level Three practice to overcome a waiting list problem that had been plaguing our service for years. When I worked in mental health, our therapy service had stubbornly high waiting lists at eight to twelve weeks in all geographical territories. I had a sense that the field was wanting to provide us with an answer. A connection was calling out to be made. I therefore spent about an hour with my therapy manager, Andrew, taking him through the theory of waiting list management and improvement technologies. I told him that an answer was close, but that I hadn't yet connected with it. It was a Tuesday. I told him to come back on Friday because I knew in my heart that he would connect with the answer by then. Before he left my office, I stopped him. 'Andrew, imagine the answer is a sphere', I said. 'Imagine that everybody who has ever attempted to tackle this problem has come from this side of the sphere. Don't go anywhere near that side. Come to it from the opposite direction. There you will find the answer.'

Two days later, not even using the three I had given him, Andrew came back to my office. The answer had found him in a flash. I hadn't known the answer but I had felt the field containing the answer had been transmitted through me to Andrew via resonance. I had Absolute Certainty that Andrew would connect with the answer and he did.

This is because all that you ever need, or that you have ever needed is already within you and always has been. This is what fuels Absolute Certainty - the knowledge that all you have to do is reach out and connect with the answer which already exists.

Anyhow, the answer in this case turned out to be stunningly, almost stupidly simple. It didn't feel to Andrew or me as if it was an answer that we had invented. It was as if it had been sitting dormant for a long time, just waiting for somebody with the right vibratory field to merely reach out and accept it, which is precisely what Andrew did.

The solution that came to us also had some positive spin-off benefits of smoothing out workload for the sixty or so people in his team and ensuring better flow of patients through the department. The only staff members that didn't like it were a couple of malingerers who would have to increase their workload. Conversely, there were some staff groups close to burnout whose workload would become much more reasonable as a result.

However, higher up in the hierarchy we met a surprising source of opposition. There was one particular person who operated mostly in Level One, and sometimes in Level Two, who appeared rather riled by the simplicity of our approach and the suddenness of our success. When we met to explain what we had done, Andrew and I felt her bristle with grudging resentment. I was taken aback by this; I had expected praise, but instead it felt as if a weight had been attached to our project. I felt my previous sense of levity being dragged downwards.

But she was coming from a place of envy and ego. Andrew and I were both so filled with Absolute Certainty over what we had done that her negativity seemed to bounce off us. Indeed, we felt a degree of pity towards her. But we maintained the programme and despite her best efforts, something of a movement began to gain traction by Andrew explaining to colleagues across the region what we had done. The technique spread, and eventually became accepted practice everywhere. There are now no community therapy waiting lists in the region.

This is indeed, a mild example of opposition to change that comes about through connecting to the preternatural field of possibility that you will experience at Level Three. I had even greater opposition when implementing another change programme that came to me a couple of years ago in a flash – a download of information that contained detailed, quite complex instructions about how to reintegrate a system into local processes that previously had been managed centrally at a distance. The staff operating in the central team were so wedded to existing processes that we didn't just experience mild opposition; we actually had to overcome quite overt sabotage to our programme of change.

So what do you do when operating at the transcendent level but you are confronted with people operating from lower levels of ego and negativity who seek to pull you back down to confront you at those levels? You have to maintain your vision, focus and knowledge at Third Level. You need to be ruthlessly focussed on seeing the big picture, the big deal. Continue to come from a place of love. Maintain your gaze upon the horizon; feel into the end result of what will manifest through your programme and synchronise your vibrations with the good that will come from it. Never engage on the level from which the opposition emanates, because it will inevitably pull you down.

In the examples given above, I knew that patients would variously wait less time in less pain, and also get out of hospital quicker to continue their rehabilitation back home. So I began with the end in mind. By asking myself, 'what will come from this programme?', I was reminded of the reason for doing what we were doing, and the reason was ultimately to give vulnerable people a better life. In this case therefore, the end result is filled with nothing but goodness. My motivation is driven by love and compassion for patients that I will never even know.

In your practice at Third Level, love always sits centre stage. So in the face of opposition, you have two choices. You can either fall down from the level of the transcendent and fight from the same vibrational field from which your opposition is attempting to fight you, or you can choose to remain in the heart of love at Third Level. When you do the latter, as it is such a different fundamental dimension to the egoic level, you will begin to find that the opposition barely registers with you any longer.

If two people are fighting a petty battle of power and politics in the same base dimensional field, you find that both receive heavy blows. It's a painful experience. But if somebody is firing arrows at you from within a dimension that you no longer inhabit, you will see and acknowledge the arrows but their power has gone. Your translucent quality at the higher vibrational dimension of Level Three gives the arrows no solid body to hit any longer. Again and eternally, the heart of love will always overcome.

We can now summarise the fifth dimension of Transcendent Leadership, which forms the first cyclical dimension: When you connect with your purpose and with those around you through the heart of love, you will experience divine flow in and through you, which will preternaturally charge your leadership practice.

Summary of Practices and Reflections in this dimension:

- Heart of Compassion   132

- Revelation, Motivation and Leverage 133

- Spirit of Love   133

- Energy Flow   142

- Connecting Compass Questions   142-143

- Dynamic Presencing   148

Chapter 6

The Sixth Dimension: Creating

Opening to Infinite Possibility

We talk a lot about disruptive technology nowadays. To engage in this level of thinking necessitates removing the metaphorical ceiling that sits above our heads. At Second Level, the ceiling is shifted upwards. At Third Level, it is removed altogether.

When stealth technology was introduced into the U.S. Air Force, the top brass in the USAF petitioned Congress to stop the research. Their world view was to procure ever faster and more manoeuvrable aircraft. Stealthy aircraft were slightly slower and slightly less manoeuvrable, ergo they were counter-strategic by nature. But their petitions were resisted as the more enlightened politicians could see what the leaders stuck at First and Second Levels couldn't see - that there was a whole new world view that they had never considered before, that of almost invisible aircraft! Now we can look back on that petition to Congress with wry amusement.

If this demonstrates a shift of thinking at Second Level, how much greater can be our shift at Third Level? What is preventing us from making that shift? Well, inertia and resistance for a start!

When I start a coaching relationship in Awakening Coaching with a new client, I write them a short letter. In it, I give them some tips of things to be aware of from the beginning. Here is the number one tip, which is based upon material from Arjuna Ardagh:

> "...anticipate resistance:
> Everyone deep down has a longing to wake up from the trance of thinking about life, and to step fully into living it. But we are all also, to some degree, at the effect of unexamined beliefs that kidnap attention and convince us that they are true. It has been my observation in working with so many people that the more we focus on awakening to our true potential, the more we also will meet resistance from the old habits of the mind. Knowing how to anticipate and move through this resistance is what determines whether breakthroughs into awakening are a fleeting "high" or a sustained way of meeting every moment."

Resistance, dear reader, is not to be underestimated. It is a very, very powerful force in your life. Resistance often comes in the form of simple boredom, or falling back on old ways of Transactional Leadership, for example, sailing through a day doing routine work – going to meetings, doing e-mails, catching up on messages and so on. One of the best ways of overcoming resistance is to crank up your curiosity, your childish belief in the adventure of discovery, the infinite possibilities of life.

For me, curiosity is one of the key inputs into my life in general. I am an endlessly curious person. I have three girls. We don't have many rules in our family, as I don't like rules much. But we do try to have principles. And one of the key principles that we have is to live a life filled with curiosity. If we did have rules, one of them would be that you are never allowed to say that you are bored. In fact, if my girls do ever say that, I either say to them, 'Andersons are never bored', or I sing, 'I'm Bored' by Iggy Pop. The latter is maybe the best way of stopping them, as it's just so irritating (to them at least – I love the song!).

Anyhow, one of the key reasons for the centrality of curiosity as a principle in our family is simply that this world is absolutely infinitely interesting. You could live a thousand lifetimes and never get to the end of learning, be it in the fields of travel, philosophy, languages, science, the arts...anything! It simply never ends. And this is the key to overcoming resistance - the curious mind cannot be bored. The curious mind, when exposed to the riches of life at the level of transcendence finds it really difficult to return to the mundane of the Transactional Level.

As with so much in this book, there are three levels of curiosity. The first level is, 'I don't know anything about this but neither do I want to' – that's level one, 'Ignorance'. This equates to Unconscious Surrender (Chapter 4).

The second level is 'I don't know but I'd like to know, I'm curious. I can discover this one for myself'. This equates to Conscious Control, again from Chapter 4. This is a necessary level or staging post in your journey towards Transcendent Leadership. This is where you actively seek out answers to things that might inspire you, or paradoxes that you try to unravel using the power of conscious thought. Sometimes ideas that are new to you, or management theories might pique your curiosity. You will then read up about them and see how they might apply to your field of work. This has happened many times in my career. Examples of theories that I have heard about have led me to buy such books as 'The Toyota Way' by Jeffrey Liker; 'Super Brain' by Deepak Chopra; and 'Polarity Management' by Barry Johnson. This level of curiosity is absolutely vital. It opens your mind up to new perspectives, new approaches, new techniques. Without it, we are just an empty vessel.

However, the third level of curiosity is the one where, as ever, the numinous magic happens. It's the one where we don't know the answer, and we know that the answer will not be found in a book. This is where our curiosity leads to 'universal flow' and 'downloads', again, outlined in chapter four.

As with the various levels of leadership, this level is just one up but it's a whole different universe from Second Level. This is because rather than relying on our own resources, we are literally opening up to the entire universe. At this level, we are merely the vehicle, the vessel through which the universe flows. We open up to the universe of infinite creativity, infinite possibility. This works best if taken to extremes, surrendering up everything that you think that you know, and releasing fear about everything that you think that you don't know.

Try this as a practice:
Go into meditation. You can use any of your favourite methods for this, or you might like to take some inspiration from my free meditation videos at www.awakeningcoaching.co.uk.
Begin by repeatedly saying to yourself, 'I know absolutely nothing. I know nothing about anything. I surrender everything that is in my mind. I totally and unreservedly open my heart to Spirit. I fully, totally

open my heart to the infinite possibilities of the universe. I align with the divine.'

Repeat this to yourself as many times as you feel is right.

As I have said before, do not push. If you push, then you bring ego into play. Rather, just *align*. Align with the Divine...do not push the Divine! You never need to push. Indeed, in my experience, when you push, absolutely nothing comes of it. Instead, it should feel more like a gentle zephyr, an opening, an affirmation. This will create a knowingness inside you. You will receive divine guidance that may appear as a download, or a nudge, or a (spiritually designed) co-incidence. It may happen immediately, or it could take a little time. Again, do not be concerned. Be patient. Just know that once you surrender and step out of the way, Spirit will respond. It may not be in the way that you expect, so throw all expectations out of the window as well. But do know that the moment you ask from the heart, Spirit has already heard.

So Second Level is limited because it leads with the head. Third Level, the level of Transcendence, always puts the heart at the forefront. Again, I would invite you to go to my website and go to the Meditations section. There you will find some beautiful, expansive practices that you can do to fan the flames of the heart and come into natural presence. Meditation is a cumulative practice – the more you practice, the more effect it appears to have in opening up the heart. If the spiritual heart were a real muscle, doing meditations daily would be like taking it to the gym. It's a beautiful and a powerful change agent.

When you make this shift from leading with the mind to moving into the heart centre and letting this be the vehicle by which you become a practitioner of Transcendent Leadership, you open up a channel through which Spirit flows.

Before I wrote my first book, I already knew something about universal flow. I hadn't yet experienced much of it, but I was soon to find out...my wife, Isabel, had gone to visit her family in South America for three weeks. My children were still young enough to go to bed at a decent time. It left me with about three hours every evening to write. The book, 'Mind-Spirit Detox', is a book of practices. Every night, I sat down on the sofa, switched the lights down low so that I felt cocooned in the world of writing, and simply opened up to the flow of the universe. It helps that I can touch-type, so there was no barrier between the flow and my laptop, but even so, I felt almost as if I were half-detached from the work such was the power of Spirit flowing through me. Of course, I was writing from a certain level of knowledge, experience and expertise. Nonetheless, I felt more like the witness of the creativity than the source of it.

I did this every evening. On days where I felt resistance, I tapped into the intelligence of 'willpower' and I just made the first steps. I told myself that all I was going to do was to sit, open the laptop and leave it at that. But once I'd done this, the tap was opened to flow, and I began to write.

Let me pause here a moment as this technique is similar to a fabulous practice for overcoming procrastination and resistance that I learnt from a friend of mine, Howard. Howard is a business school professor, teaching on one of the UK's foremost MBA courses. He lives around ten minutes walk from the Virgin gym near St Paul's Cathedral in central London. Being the same age as me, fast approaching his 50th birthday at the time of writing, he and I both like to attempt to stay in shape, otherwise the inevitable slide into middle age will accelerate towards us faster than we might like. But like many people, Howard finds that resistance and self-sabotage often creep in when he knows he really ought to go the gym.

Howard's technique for overcoming this is *not* to say to himself that he is going to walk or run to the gym, do an hour's workout and then walk back. No! This is too much to overcome when resistance is high. Instead, he just tells himself that he will put on his gear, go out of the door and walk in the direction of the gym. That's it. Simple. All he makes himself do is to take the first steps. When he's walking towards the gym, he then tends to start to run. And then when he reaches the gym, he inevitably warms up and gets on the first piece of equipment. And once he's there, he's into it and he finishes the session.

So next time you feel resistance and self-sabotage bubbling up, try this practice. Just make yourself do the first thing that you have to in that exercise. You will inevitably find that you complete it.

Anyhow, back to the writing of my book. Knowing Howard's exercise, I'd either want to write or I at least made myself a drink, sat down on the sofa and opened my laptop. First steps. Then, as soon as I got in front of the laptop, magic happened. I entered into the flow state (Mihály Csíkszentmihályi coined this phrase in 1975, meaning the mental state where one is 'in the zone', fully immersed in an activity to the point where everything else effectively disappears, even the sense of time). Yes, it was me doing the typing and there was a degree of thought involved, but the creativity was simply bubbling up from another source, a source outside of me.

When flow is switched on, there is little of thought and mind involved. The mind is more used to review and nudge. Creativity however, comes from Source. To me I always feel as if it is something flowing from above my head, coming down through the top of the head (some people might describe this as the crown chakra), and flowing through my body, through my heart and out through my fingers. I become more of an observer, a witness to this remarkable process that still staggers me to this day.

When I am leading my team, again, I feel the same kind of flow. This time often it feels much broader and the connection with my team is more like a river. I have a gift known as clairecognizance. I receive this absolute knowledge of the right questions to ask in supervision and the right avenue down which they need to be walking. I just know with Absolute Certainty what the Universe has in store for them, the gift that matches their genius. Again, this comes through me as a river of creative flow, divinely inspired. This is what happens when you surrender and open to Spirit. When you practice these gifts in a leadership context, you can truly call yourself a Transcendent Leader.

Each of us has a certain gift that is the perfect one for us. So many coaches, for instance, seem to have the gift of clairecognizance as I do. People with this tell me that whatever comes through them is the perfect question or nudge or answer that the person being coached needs at that moment. Or if they are speaking in public, the perfect lines come out of their mouth. It's about surrendering ego, opening up a channel and having Spirit speak through you.

The process of creation therefore, is leveraged a thousand-fold or more through the process of opening yourself to the gifts of spirit, the birthright that awaits you in the field of the numinous. But this is just about your own gifts as a leader. So what about the rest of the team?

As in the words of Steve Jobs, you are merely the conductor of the orchestra *("The musicians play their instruments, I play the orchestra")*. As a leader you are not expected to try to play all of the instruments at the same time. Indeed, you are not playing any of the instruments. How ridiculous would the conductor look if he or she were both conducting as well as trying to help the orchestra out by playing the tuba at the same time! Moreover, it would detract from the unique contribution that the conductor is bringing to the overall 'team' – that of direction, maintaining coherence and injecting art and inspiration.

How many leaders fall at this most basic of hurdles? I have already mentioned that I see my leadership role as attracting and retaining brilliant people, then creating a framework by which those brilliant people can be brilliant. There isn't much more to it than that! I am not trying to play all of the instruments, although I do have to know how they all work, what their possibilities and limitations are, and how best to create a cohesive whole.

So if we leverage our own abilities by opening up to subtle energies, gifts and universal flow, how then do we leverage the power and brilliance of our team? Well, we need to be able to transmit the creativity and abundance that is now flowing through us to our top team plus all of the people underneath them. One of the key mechanisms that I use in my practice for this is what for a long time I took to be the placebo effect.

In medicine, the placebo effect describes the positive results that follow from taking medicine that has no direct pharmacological effects. The appearance of the tablet has a marked effect on the power of the placebo, according to the degree of face-validity it has. Therefore two tablets have a greater placebo effect than one tablet alone. The colour of the pill is important, too. It appears that green pills have more effect for relieving anxiety; blue pills are more effective for helping people to sleep. If the tablet has something printed on it, it has yet more effect. If it is in a capsule form the effect is again increased. If administered as an injection, even more so. Finally, placebo surgery sometimes has even more of a positive effect than actual surgery itself [*Moseley JB, O'Malley K, Petersen NJ, et al. "A controlled trial of arthroscopic surgery for osteoarthritis of the knee"*]

Medical trials always include a double blind test to attempt to rule out the placebo effect. This is whereby the actual drug and a tablet that does not contain the drug are administered to two groups of patients respectively. Neither the researcher nor the patients know which is which.

The importance of screening out the placebo effect cannot be over-emphasised. The effect seems to be becoming more and more powerful over time. Nobody is quite sure why. What seems certain, however, is that the placebo demonstrates just how powerful the mind and expectations are in delivering physiological results. And if harnessing the power of your mind can have such profound effects on the body, think just how powerful it is when the mind is brought into the field of leadership.

As expectations can affect outcomes in medicine, the same mechanism applies in a leadership context. This is, again, where Absolute Certainty comes in. The greatest gift we can give our clients or our staff is the Absolute Certainty that they already have everything that they need to be who they need to be. If I as a coach have Absolute Certainty, then the client will also have Absolute Certainty. This is one of the most powerful mechanisms that I know. It is transmitted from me to the client. Every time. Without fail. I have never, ever, known this not to work.

In the same way, in my leadership practice, whenever I interact with anybody in my team, I transmit Absolute Certainty to them. At one level, the mechanism of transmission can be considered to be akin to the placebo effect. People in my team see that I know what I am saying with every fibre of my being. And they too then know. So when I tell teams that we are the best performing team in our region, guess what happens? We become the best team in the region. Indeed, on what is perhaps our most important Key Performance Indicator, i.e. preventing unnecessary hospital admissions, we are perhaps the best performing team in all of England. This is simply incredible. On top of that, we are in many respects, the least well resourced team in our region. As a consequence, we are the most efficient.

So how have we done it? Well, my team has been liberated to be the best version of themselves, to let their creative brilliance fly. So they have themselves designed some simple yet highly effective systems and processes. But surrounding all of this is the Absolute Certainty that they have of their being an off-the-scale brilliant team. And this comes from my own Absolute Certainty that they are an off-the-scale brilliant team.

However, the placebo effect only serves to explain so much. I now know it to be a factor in transmitting Absolute Certainty, but I believe it now to be the smaller part of a much bigger, more powerful phenomenon that is at work at Third Level.

When you awaken to spirit, you resonate powerful signals out into the Akashic Field (this is a theoretical field of information that Ervin Lásló suggests holds all consciousness and information). Your consciousness, your awakened energy, activates the field around you and this in turn activates awakening in those around you. This activation is transmitted to those around you via resonance, hence I call it 'resonant transmission'.

Let me break this down. 'Transmission' speaks for itself. I use the word, 'resonance' because it is similar to the notion of *'sympathetic resonance'*. This is defined as 'a harmonic phenomenon wherein a formerly passive string or vibratory body responds to external vibrations to which it has a harmonic likeness.' For example, the strings of a violin will begin to vibrate when a tuning fork is struck and placed nearby.

Tune in yourself to the frequencies and vibration of Spirit and if you act out of love and integrity, the effect on those around you can only be described as magical.

You may have heard the quote by the science fiction writer, Arthur C. Clarke, 'Any sufficiently advanced technology is indistinguishable from magic.' Well I can tell you in similar vein, that any sufficiently skilled practitioner of Transcendent Leadership produces an effect on his or her organisation that is indistinguishable from magic.

The self-fulfilling prophecy was never so powerful. Never ever underestimate the power of resonant transmission in your leadership practice. What you give out in terms of words, deeds, knowledge and vision truly manifests into day-to-day reality.

I see the resonance effect of Absolute Certainty in one of my favourite sports - Formula 1. There are some fabulous lessons that we can learn from a couple of their teams. Let's have a look at how they use some Level Two tools and weave them into Level Three outcomes.

Firstly, McLaren, a UK team based in Woking just outside London. They expanded from mostly making just Formula 1 cars to latterly include a road car division. They are constantly improving and innovating as a car company. I once heard an executive explain how they tapped into creativity and encouraged all employees to come up with innovative solutions. When they did this, they then tested ideas against three key Second Level rules, thus:

> ➢ Does it fit with our philosophy?

- Do we have the technology/capacity/capability to produce/deliver it?
- Will the customer buy it? (i.e. is there demand for it?)

Another top Formula 1 team, in fact, the top team at time of writing, is Mercedes, who also use three simple rules as a springboard into Level Three. The team is led by the inspirational Toto Wolf. He was recently interviewed following their best ever start to a season; this following five straight years of constructors championships. "How do you maintain such incredible focus?", asked the interviewer. "Two things.", said Toto. "Firstly, we haven't lost our top people to rival teams. Normally when teams win a lot, their employees become very valuable to the other teams. They have knowledge that the others want to tap into. So they can then earn more elsewhere. They are poached. And this is true of us. Other teams try to poach our staff with lucrative offers. But they stay, they are not tempted. Why? Because we have what they will not be able to get elsewhere. The best possible team atmosphere within which to work and further their career. No other team offers the thing that we have going here at Mercedes. Secondly and most importantly, we never, ever rest. Even if we come 1-2 in a race, we have the same routine after every finish. The team all meets together in a safe space and we debrief. We always start with our shortcomings even if we were amazing. There is always something that we can improve upon. Then we do three things: see, say, fix. It goes like this:

- See it: what did you see today?
- Say it: be open about it. What could be improved?
- Fix it: act on it. Never leave a situation unimproved."

There you have it. A habit developed over years of racing together, which consists of three rules – you see it, you say it, you fix it. And through this Level Two habit, something in Level Three happened that was extraordinary, magical even. The entire team began to break records left right and centre. Whilst Toto Wolf spoke of how they had achieved this in a spirit of 'modesty and humility', Ferrari, the perpetual underdog in this period, puffed and panted, sacked team boss after team boss, even got sanctioned by the FIA (the governing body) for irregularities and ultimately lost year after year.

As in the words of William Arthur Ward, "The mediocre teacher tells. The good teacher explains. The superior teacher demonstrates. The great teacher inspires.", and so too does Mercedes. Indeed, what could be more inspirational than their pithy mission statement, 'The best or nothing'. For them and for other teams who have made contact with their source of inspiration, they are able to simply hold their meaning in a few short words.

Toto Wolf has created a field around his team that has a lot of features at Level Three. He displays Absolute Certainty that his team will come out on top. In him you see no wobbles or doubt when it comes to the macro picture. Sure, he will admit that things don't go to plan every week, but even if the team have an off day, he is still certain about the bigger picture, that no other team can offer what Mercedes offers.

Thus we can see that some effortless rules and techniques in Level Two can unlock powerful frequencies at Level Three, if applied with the correct frequency and intention. I call these techniques that sit at the cusp of Level Three, 'liminal practices'. They occupy the space between one level and the other. For those people who are starting out on the spiritual path, who are perhaps not yet fully comfortable about using subtle energies and spiritual techniques, it can be a great way to access the transcendent space.

Closely related to the Mercedes rules is another liminal practice, a technique around problem solving. It's simple. Always simple – Do this every time and you'll never be left with a festering problem. Take your problem and then choose one of only three options:
1) Fix it
2) Live with it
3) Walk away from it

There is no fourth option: 'procrastinate/none of the above' is NOT an option. This is fabulous! It probably straddles the border between Level Two and Level Three, but never forget that as a Transcendent Leader, you need to continue to practice at all three levels. They are all necessary. What I do know for certain is that if you don't act from present awareness, then your conditioned self often puts impediments in your own way to breaking through and maintaining focus in Level Three. If you choose the forth option here, you will be doing just that.

Another company, not far from where I live, located in Salisbury, England, is 'Naim'. They produce HiFi equipment of the highest calibre. Their reason for existence is summed up thus: "Every Naim product is conceived, designed and engineered entirely in service of the sound, revealing a pure experience of music that is as close as possible to its original live source." So the source of their inspiration comes again, as it does with Mercedes, from four words, in this case, 'pure experience of music'.

Thus we can see that insight, creativity and inspiration can emerge through the application of simple rules when applied with the right frequency. Ralph Waldo Emerson once said, "Our chief want is someone who will inspire us to be what we know we could be."

So challenge yourself. What is your inspiration? Could you describe your inspiration in four words? Spend some time right now contemplating this. If you were to look back at your life on your deathbed and see the thing that you had come to earth to do, what would it have been?

If you were explaining to a grandchild what you did with your life, and you wanted to convey to them every last drop of excitement and inspiration you had for the thing that you led, how would you tell them? Get this right and your work is no longer merely a job to do – rather, it is a mission to accomplish. You then start living for the mission.

If you haven't already done this inner work, I would urge you to spend time now contemplating it so that you can fully understand what has meaning to you in your life. Find the alignment. When you connect with it, you will soon find that everybody around you also begins to connect with it through resonance. Abundance and creativity will spring forth from the field that you co-create together.

Openness, flow, surrender and creativity are key to aligning our inner motivations with the outer expression

of those motivations. Imagination is the fuel behind all of these factors. Just think about it for a moment - everything ever created has been first been imagined. We can absolutely control the future from our imagination in the present moment. Some people stuck at Levels One or Two might struggle with the notion that we really can affect the future through imagination. However, this isn't just fanciful philosophy but is actually rooted in emergent understandings of science.

The world at a fundamental level, the level of quantum, is way more strange than our puny minds can even begin to comprehend. To illustrate this, let's look at what Einstein called, 'spooky action at a distance'. It has been suggested from within the field of quantum physics that our imagination can even change the past itself. In other words, causation can run backwards as well as forwards. This is because particles do not operate like solid billiard balls bashing into each other on a table. Rather, they are like blurry clouds of possibilities shifting in space. Physicists have long been intrigued by whether this cloud of possibilities is actually just representational or if it is real. They wanted to know whether the strangeness at quantum level also worked when it came to notions of time. In 2018, Mike Mcrae summarised this in a paper entitled, 'This Quantum Theory Predicts that the Future Might be Influencing the Past'. Here is what he says:

"Matthew S. Leifer from Chapman University in California and Matthew F. Pusey from the Perimeter Institute for Theoretical Physics in Ontario...exchanged some of Price's assumptions and applied their new model to something called Bell's theorem, which is a big deal in this whole spooky action at a distance business.

John Stewart Bell said that the weird things that happen in quantum mechanics can't ever be explained by actions taking place nearby. It's as if nothing is causing the multitude of billiard balls to take such varied paths. At a fundamental level, the Universe is random.

But what about actions taking place somewhere else... or some*when* else? Can something far away influence that cloud without touching it, in a way that Einstein called "spooky"?

If two particles are connected in space at some point, measuring a property of one of them instantly sets the value for the other, no matter where in the Universe it has moved to. This 'entanglement' has been tested over and over again in light of Bell's theorem, plugging loopholes that might show they are really interacting on a local level in some way, in spite of what seems to be a distance.

As you might guess, the Universe still seems pretty spooky.

But if causality ran backwards, it would mean a particle could carry the action of its measurement back in time to when it was entangled, affecting its partner. No faster-than-light messages needed....In any case, the idea of anything trickling backwards in time might not be an appealing one, but let's face it, when it comes to phenomena like entanglement, nearly any explanation is going to sound downright insane."

The physics of backward imagination is far from settled, but the basic fact remains that it is almost impossible to comprehend from our small and partial view of the world. The great physicist Richard Feynman once delivered a lecture entitled, 'The Character of Physical

Law', in which he said, 'If you think you understand quantum mechanics, you don't understand quantum mechanics'. He later added, 'I think I can safely say that nobody understands quantum mechanics.'

The point I am reaching for is really that the very notion of 'transcendence' in leadership is at this point in our understanding effectively boundless, and our view can only be partial. When it comes to creativity, we can only begin to understand the mechanics at work. Moreover, if there's even a possibility that our imagination can potentially affect time and events in reverse, think how much more probable is the notion of our imagination and creativity affecting outcomes in the *future*.

So do not stop imagining! When you truly believe and feel that what you are imagining is true, you are ensuring your success in bringing what you imagine into manifest reality. When you get this right; when your imagination is in alignment with the universe, you will have a feeling of 'rightness' that corroborates that feeling. The feeling will corroborate the belief. This is an absolutely important and necessary part of the imagination-manifestation cycle. When that feeling emerges, you must magnify it and live the feeling. Feel it with all of you – with your mind, your thoughts, your body. Make the feeling so alive as to trigger an emotional reaction within you. Feel into the emotion as if what you have is your present reality, not just some future 'maybe'.

Hold onto the emotion and the feeling and magnify that emotion and you will be hooking into the quantum field of possibility. It's as if you are letting billiard balls emerge from the fug of the quantum soup. The blurry cloud of possibility collapses down into definitive, material matter. The things that emerge are the product of what we have imagined and felt prior to it manifesting. Reality becomes potential form from imagination and that potential form becomes guaranteed or locked in as a result of the expansion of emotion.

Intentionality, clarity, specificity are all also vital in creating focus to what emerges. Form derives from the formless. And let me make it clear that what emerges is given unimaginable leverage if you establish a framework whereby your entire team taps into this field of possibility. The Third Level Leader instinctively knows that they have to empower their team to establish this leverage. But it can be a scary moment to really seek to empower people due to the ego's propensity to feel as if it is ceding control to others.

As such, a useful mechanism that I have practised for many years is, 'freedom within a framework'. This paradoxically can increase freedom for team members because they are given the boundaries within which they can operate.

> "The greatest leader is not necessarily the one who does the greatest things. He is the one that gets the people to do the greatest things."
>
> *Ronald Reagan*

Without boundaries, people can become frozen – a paralysis of too much choice. With them, they begin to move and explore. Choose your boundaries wisely. Ensure that they fit in with organisational imperatives; ensure that they are wide enough to allow creativity to flourish but not so wide as to effectively have no framework.

Down the years, I have used frameworks such as:
- You can move revenue to capital but not capital to revenue. Beyond this, as long as your bottom right hand balance isn't overspent, you can do what you like with the budget.
- Freedom to make common sense decisions as long as they are risk assessed and not reckless.
- Freedom to make decisions without constantly having to check back with me.

I have even gone so far as to say that I will not (metaphorically) kick people's back sides for making an honest decision in good faith, but that I will kick people's back sides for trying to cover their back sides by continually asking for permission. That's not what I hire people for – I hire them to use their brains and their professional judgement! In the words of Theodore Roosevelt, "The best executive is the one who has sense enough to pick good men to do what he wants done, and self-restraint to keep from meddling with them while they do it."

Remember, to truly hit cruising altitude at Level Three, you select brilliant people and then create a framework of empowerment that enables those brilliant people to be brilliant. It is the combination of personal mastery and the correct level of autonomy that makes potentially merely ordinary people become extraordinary. It's what shifts a team from going through the motions at Level One to creating a world of infinite possibility at Level Three.

We are now in a position to summarise the sixth dimension of Transcendent Leadership thus: When you tune in to the frequencies and vibration of Spirit, infinite possibility and creativity arises spontaneously and is activated in those around you via resonant transmission.

Summary of Practices and Reflections in this dimension:

- Curiosity   158

- Flow state   161

- Overcoming Self-Sabotage   162

- Inspiration in Four Words   172

- Imagination-manifestation cycle   175

- Freedom within a Framework   177

Chapter 7

The Seventh Dimension: Doing

Manifesting

We spoke earlier of developing the flow state, the moment when we step aside and we allow the universe to manifest through us. When this flow begins, we will start to feel a radical power, a radiance, surrounding us.

Think for a minute of the people in your team who also give off radiance when they walk in the room. People who, when they speak, bring a sense of uplift to those around them. As a Transcendent Leader, it is vital that you carefully and deliberately nurture these people. Be very conscious of this. If it has not yet occurred to you who these people are, then this next week, be aware of it and feel into it. You may be surprised by who it is giving off this numinous quality. Those people who really shine are what I call 'Light Workers'.

Conversely, in my experience, it is close to impossible to practise Transcendent Leadership if you are surrounded by people that emit the opposite quality. Those people that are eternally stressed, critical, afraid, controlling and ego-driven. Such people are like a vortex of negative energy. They walk into a room and suck the life out of it. Such people will tell you to 'cover your back'; 'take no risks'; they will whinge and complain. It's here where tough love sometimes comes into play.

My default position with such people is to come alongside them, understand their problems and see if I can bring them with me on the development path we are on as a team. It is rare for this not to work. However, the leader within an organisation really cannot afford a level of infinite patience. We have goods and services to deliver. In my estimation, there are always around one to two percent of workers who are simply poisonous to a team and to an organisation. Such people lack interpersonal and intrapersonal intelligence. They come from a position of lack, of fear, of control. And when they are put into any kind of leadership position, the only people they attract in their teams are like-minded individuals. For the vast majority, such people create disempowerment, sickness and oppression.

As a leader, I have absolutely no truck with these people. I do everything I can to shift their resonance, but ultimately their choice is to improve, or to ship out. Over the course of my career, I have managed teams of between 300 and nearly 2,000 people. In that time, I have parted ways with about 12-15 people. The clear-out was probably front-loaded towards the beginning of that time. Nobody has left for a couple of years now; I hope that we're learning how to better recruit people with the requisite EQ ability.

Note: Emotional Intelligence, or emotional quotient (EQ), is defined as an person's ability to understand, acknowledge/identify, evaluate, control, and then to express emotions. This is distinct from IQ, or intelligence quotient, which is a score derived from one of several standardized tests designed to assess an individual's cognitive intelligence.

An example of this was a team leader I managed when I worked in a finance department who led a team of about 25 people. As my leadership philosophy became better known and trusted, a few brave souls came to me and expressed regret that what I was expounding wasn't present in their team. They said that their manager was a bully who kept them in their place. One day, this manager was observed doing supervision the other side of a glass wall. She could be seen thumping the desk and shouting. I moved quickly, and had an informal meeting (what I sometimes like to call a 'fireside chat') with the manager, who admitted that she could lose self-control from time to time.

She knew that she was doing it and promised not to do it again. She went further. She said that she was so serious about sorting out her problem that if she did it again, she would resign. I offered her some support with this and another discussion then I waited. Three months later, she exploded with rage once more. We met again and within a week, she resigned.

In fact, none of the people with whom I have parted ways down the years has been sacked. Only one has been subject to a formal disciplinary process. Even then they weren't sacked. They decided to leave, as did all of the others.

When we hold onto truth, when we hold onto love, when we ourselves act as beings of light, our light can shine so brightly that those people who walk in darkness are blinded. They cannot stand it. I cannot guarantee this in every case, but for the vast majority of such people, when they recognise that they are unable to spread their bile in your team or organisation, they will voluntarily leave in order to continue their negative practice somewhere else.

This is a difficult subject to write about and a difficult one to confront in a book with 'transcendent' in the title. And I must stress that for every person who has left,

I've had many, many more who I have coached into the light. However, leadership sometimes requires us to be tough, but our toughness comes from love and nowhere else.

I cannot stress enough how important it is for you to surround yourself with brilliant people, with light workers. Transcendence demands it. Your light needs to be absorbed, not repelled. Just to hammer the point home, here is my very simple but powerful guide:

- Hire brilliant people

- Develop or part ways with the others

- Your role as a Transcendent Leader is around creating a space for brilliant people to be brilliant. Period. And it begins and ends with love.

When you are able to create this magical space of brilliance, you will begin to see all of your hopes, aspirations and design work shift from the domain of the formless (your mind, your thoughts) into the world of form, the manifest realm. Manifestation is essentially this movement from thought to reality; from design into the real world.

Much has been written about manifestation of late and for a reason. It works! I will give you some examples from my own life. Firstly, my wife. I met her whilst travelling in Paraguay many years ago. I returned a couple more times to Paraguay and eventually we started dating. But it was rather like dating in name only because we were separated by an ocean and 6,500 miles. I thought it impossible. In fact, I called her 'my impossible dream'. However, I kept picturing it happening; Isabel coming to live with me in England. Eventually, many synchronicities occurred and she did indeed come to England, marry me, and now we have three beautiful daughters.

Later, I pictured what life could be like moving away from the suburbs of London and living by the sea in Devon. A few short months later, we were there. I have had many, many other such experiences of manifestation. Indeed, Isabel's own life has been one of incredible manifestation.

She was born an identical triplet into extreme poverty. She and her sisters would have died if it wasn't for the fact that their plight was shown on national news and a rich benefactor ensured that they were given good medical treatment. Isabel was surrounded with family and friends who told her that she would amount to nothing, but she in her heart always knew that her life would be different. Today she has a good managerial career in the UK and bag loads of qualifications. The people who told her that she would spend her life in poverty are doing just that – living a life of poverty. Isabel's Absolute Certainty that her life would be different created the very life that she dreamt about.

The one area of manifestation that has always stood just outside my belief zone in that it just felt too unrealistic, was that of prosperity manifestation. However, several years ago, Isabel and I for various reasons were both frustrated about our financial situation. I earn quite well but lots of bills and unforeseen expenses had been piling up and we wanted to break the cycle. So we got down to some prosperity manifestation practice. I'll list below the questions we both asked and answered.

Try this as a practice. Don't forget to write down your answers, and if you're in a relationship, try doing it as a couple.

1) Firstly, get rid of any resistance and negativity you have towards prosperity. Write down the things that you feel that get in the way, e.g. 'people will be jealous'; 'I don't deserve it', and so on. Once written down, shred the paper or burn it. Give it up. It is gone forever.

2) Write down the great things that would happen in your life if you had lots of money.

3) Write down the benefits to other people/society/the planet if you had lots of money.

4) Write down how you may get the money.

5) Write down the qualities and genius that you have which will enable this to happen.

6) Write down a sentence, starting with, 'I am grateful to money because.....', and fill in the blanks.

7) Write down how money is going to add value to your life.

8) Finally and most importantly, you need to do a very important thing. Your positive thoughts will attract 'good' to you. Money and abundance is your good - remember the aphorism, 'thoughts held in mind produce after their kind'. You have already been doing the thinking. Now turn to the feeling, the emotion.

I want you to find a comfortable place to be. Sit or lie and close your eyes. Relax. Focus on your breathing for a little while. Now I want you to picture a fantasy day in your future life. Your life of abundance. Picture it in minute detail:

What are you wearing?

Who are you with?

What are you doing?

What is around you?

Where are you?

Now run through this again and this time, sink into *feeling*. What emotions does it bring? This part is vitally important. Really explore the feelings that having what you want will elicit in you. You don't have to put it into words, just connect with the heart, with feeling.

I did this practice with Isabel, my wife. Quite remarkable things then all came together in the following month:

- We paid our mortgage off in full, and my endowment paid me an excess on top of the mortgage.

- Isabel's main job necessitated more hours and she earned multiples of her normal salary.

- Isabel got a personal training client who paid her up-front for a large package of training.

- We received a large feed-in tariff payment from our solar panels.

- I got paid royalties from my previous book.

Once we had added everything up, we had thousands of pounds more than we'd normally have. With part of the money, we have started a fund to reforest our land in Paraguay and try to safeguard some ancient forest. And we went out for a wonderful meal together as a family, a luxury we often deny ourselves.

Thus my cynical mistrust of wealth manifestation has been well and truly dispelled forever. If you would like to meditate deeper in this area, I have posted three abundance meditations on my website. Just go to: https://www.awakeningcoaching.co.uk/meditations

You can use these steps for manifesting anything that you like, not just money. I have used them with a coaching client who wanted to start her own business, for example. And of course, included in the list of things that you can manifest is the team or organisation for which you are responsible as a leader. The importance of this work to your success as a Transcendent Leader at the Third Level cannot be over emphasised.

What should be blindingly obvious by now to anybody paying attention to this book is that one of the key ways in which Third Level differs from Second Level is the fact that you have begun to humble yourself, step aside and allow the power of the universe to flow through you and your leadership practice. You open yourself up to tools and techniques that are divine by nature and that use emergent knowledge of how we as human beings connect with the quantum field. That's why Third Level is so radically different from First and Second. First and Second Levels depend only upon *you*. Just you. Third Level radically shifts to include the entire Universe. Now that's an order of magnitude as close to infinity as it is possible to get.

Let's get one thing straight, however. When we talk of the Universe, we're not talking about the Cosmos that is *out there,* that is somehow different and separate from you. No! The Universe, divine consciousness, already resides *within* you. You are it and it is you. It's just that most people are blind to this. You are absolutely one with the Universe. When looked at scientifically, we now know that we are actually created from atoms that were created in exploding stars. Scientists are still debating whether it is supernovas or white dwarfs that are the key source of carbon in the universe, either way, we come from the stars as carbon-based life forms. We are inherently of the stars, the universe – it's not merely a metaphor.

From a Biblical perspective, Jesus told the Pharisees that the Kingdom of Heaven is within us (Luke 17:21). *Within us* – not somewhere else, not in some distant place that is far off or hidden, but absolutely and irrefutably part of your very being right here, right now.

We are therefore simply talking about tapping into what is already there, and which has always been there and which always will be there. This power is immense, should we just open our eyes and see it!

So I would absolutely implore you to do this manifestation exercise in the full knowledge that you have all the resources of The Divine at your disposal. And once you have done that, I would like you to turn your attention towards manifesting brilliance within your team. Here's how.

Turn away from any preconceived notions of yourself as an heroic leader. Dump those egoic thoughts firmly in the bin. Instead, see yourself in truth as a channel for manifestation. Understand also that the thing that you are manifesting is ultimately the goods or the services that your team or organisation provides. However, do not fall into the trap of being ruthlessly focussed on the end product. Sure, know what you are looking to produce. Plan it; decide where in the economy or society it will be placed; get the design right; get the costs right; create the networks and the buzz.

All of these things belong to First and Second Levels, i.e. the Transactional and Transformational realms. Do not forget that the Third Level, Transcendent Leadership, is built upon these first two levels. So they are a vitally important pre-condition to mastering Third Level. Get them right. However, we're talking Transcendence here and the key to manifesting brilliance of product or service at this level is not to maintain your entire focus on the outcomes themselves; it's to create the conditions for transcendence in the inputs – in the people around you, in the team, in the organisation.

You have to realise that even if you fully understand and absorb this whole transcendent paradigm, not everybody in your organisation will. It's a movement, and unfortunately, some people just are not ready for it. When people see something new and exciting happening in you and in those around you, they will change. Theories abound around this, such as those I have already mentioned in the book, for example, as the hundred monkeys theory, and Ken Wilber's 'tipping points'. Additionally, in academic literature, there are a whole host of theoretical paradigms of movements from 'Social Movement Impact Theory' to 'Resource Mobilisation Theory' to 'Political Process Theory' which you can study at your leisure.

The truth as I have experienced it is that you will begin to see a trickle of people simply hooking naturally into your way of thinking. Then a few more, then a few more. As I've touched on already, Spiral Dynamic theorists assert that when around ten percent of any population achieve an evolutionary step to a new level of understanding, suddenly the entire population get it. How that happens hardly matters, but it is useful to have a degree of familiarity with the underlying theory of movements and transmission because it helps you to dispel doubt in your ability to take your team with you. There are fabulous theories that explain the mechanics behind transmission such as that which I briefly mentioned, Ervin Laszlo's Akashic Field theory; Rupert Sheldrake's Morphic Resonance and so on.

Sheldrake argues that that not all information is contained within our brains. Instead, our brains and indeed body act like a radio receiver. We operate more like streaming machines than a Blu-ray player or CD player. Information resides in the Akashic field or the Morphic field rather than in our heads. This is how psychic phenomena work. My interest in this was piqued as my wife, being an identical triplet, is able to feel the pain of her sisters who live in South America. Indeed, the minute Isabel gave birth to my youngest daughter, one of her sisters, at the time childless, began lactating. On another occasion, Isabel visited the dentist because one of her molars was hurting her terribly. The dentist proclaimed that there was absolutely nothing wrong with the tooth. When she got home and told me, I suggested that she contact her sisters. One of them had been to the dentist herself that day as she had an abscess in it – the very same tooth as the one that had been troubling Isabel!

Theories around where information is stored and transmitted in this way are not new. I mentioned earlier a precursor to Laszlo and Sheldrake's work in the book by Jeremy Campbell, 'Grammatical Man: Information, Entropy, Language and Life'. What Sheldrake and

Laszlo did in terms of building on this work was to bring in new developments in quantum mechanics, especially the mechanisms of quantum entanglement and quantum non-locality, to begin to explain these phenomena.

Sheldrake is a former professor of biology at Cambridge University. He has run experiments for many years on the psychic abilities of domestic cats and dogs. His theories also explain starling murmuration, where up to 100,000 birds can fly almost in unison. Sheldrake explains that the movements between birds are so instantaneously co-ordinated that existing bio-mechanical explanations go nowhere near answering just how this phenomena can manifest. When you hook into Sheldrake's work, you begin to see examples of it all over the place. Having at least an intuitive understanding of the theory of social movements and the transmission mechanisms for them is really key to expansion of your practice.

I have always been somewhat cautious in my field of work about explaining to other people some of the possible theoretical frameworks and the knowledge and revelations that lie behind Transcendent Leadership practice. Bringing esoteric fields of study into organisations is not exactly mainstream yet and there is just too much of a prevailing culture of reductionism and philosophical materialism for them to get much traction in most work-places. However, it seems to me that little by little increasing numbers of people are accepting of this emergent field of knowledge.

Whatever the mechanisms, people have most definitely noticed far and wide that there is something marvellously different about my team. I have even had politicians whose brief it is to oversee my work, make a bee-line to my office to quiz me about the theories that drive my leadership practice, because they see such benefit for the rest of the county as well as the industry that they are in themselves.

I recall a time when a senior nurse who worked many years ago in my team (who had left for promotion for a number of years), returned back to the team. What she told me made me very emotional because it told me in my heart that what I had been pursuing with such vigour, was working. When I asked her how it was to be back, she told me, 'Richard, it's like coming home. This team is so happy, it's so together; we really feel like we're on fire. The passion in this team is immense.' Then she went on to say, 'I'm so lucky to be back. Do you know that people all over the county are trying to get a job in this team? Everyone knows it's the best place to work.'

Wow!

So what does all of this have to do with manifesting? The point is that all first class goods and services produced on this planet are produced by first class organisations. It is almost impossible to consistently over time produce great product if you have a moribund, feckless or dysfunctional organisation. So get the organisation right and everything will follow. It's a bit like what I heard Sir Richard Branson say, "'Clients do not come first. Employees come first. If you take care of your employees, they will take care of the clients." In the same way, your organisation comes first. That will take care of the finished product. This is the way to manifest. Through the people, through the team, through the organisation. So whenever you hear a leader say that they are ruthlessly focussed on end product, you will see a leader who is bound to fail.

Such leaders are often those who can be described as the 'heroic leader'. These are often extrovert, charismatic, bombastic 'shapers' (see Belbin teambuilding theory). All doors lead to them. They assume a command/control style, using out-dated management models such as Taylor's Scientific Management Theory. They think that they can pull on a lever and something will happen. It's based on Newtonian physics. We now know that people and organisations are more subtle and complex than that.

In fact, if we want to correlate the levels of leadership with scientific theory, then First Level (transactional) is based on Newtonian models. Second Level (transformational) is still mostly at this level, with the odd nod to something more expansive. Third Level embraces quantum understanding, relativity and also rockets on to a more holistic embrace of everything – where the manifest and esoteric realms become one, becoming an integral whole.

Indeed, when you as a leader are practising at Third Level, your team begins to operate as if it were a cohesive, integral entity in its own right. Unlike with the heroic leader model, not everything comes from you. This is because you create the conditions by which the team begins to act as an independent body, one that is no longer wholly dependent upon you being physically present at all times.

Let me illustrate this. When the command/control heroic leader goes on holiday, everything collapses. Because they have bred non-thinking, dependent, disempowered and fearful individuals, the latter are inevitably dependent upon the leader being present. It's a self-fulfilling prophecy. So when this type of leader returns from leave, they often return to a disaster zone. This then reinforces their opinion about their being indispensible.

The Transcendent Leader on the other hand has created space for brilliant people to be brilliant. When they go on holiday that space and the brilliance remains. Therefore when they return from holiday, not only has nothing collapsed, but moreover it has improved.

The people in the team are like neurons in a neuron network, the building blocks of the brain. Within the brain, information from one neuron flows to another neuron across a synapse. This is essentially what learning is. The brain has the ability to constantly change and to grow. This is known as neuroplasticity. When you practice Transcendent Leadership, you will create a team that begins to share information, to learn, to create, to connect and so on. The Transcendent Leader will see that his or her team develops its own neuroplasticity.

I once returned from leave and plunged into what could have been a difficult meeting with some reportedly disgruntled staff. We had recently taken a team on from another part of the organisation. The morale of this group of staff had taken a battering - they didn't feel listened to, and I went into the meeting feeling like a lamb going to slaughter.

This was the first time that I realised that my wider team had developed its own neuroplasticity. I was simply astonished by what I saw. When I entered the meeting room, the feel of the team wasn't what I had expected at all. There was a real buzz in the room. The staff were palpably excited and invigorated. One of my middle-ranking nurses and a therapist had been doing group supervision with them. Each team member was taking it in turns to talk about problematic and/or complex clients. The nurse and therapist were listening intently, giving feedback, coaching the staff and suggesting courses of action. There was active listening, problem-solving and learning going on.

The structure of the meeting was not my idea. It was a brilliant idea, but it didn't come from me – I'd been on holiday. Whilst I had been away, connections had been made, creativity and ideas made manifest. It had come from the learning and self-developing brain that is my team. I was the witness to manifestation at Third Level. Brilliant!

Watching this unfold before me, I realised that my team were really in the zone of transcendence. We were deep, deep down into it. This was no liminal space on the edge of transcendence, this was the real deal.

It reminded me of a time when I was training to be an Awakening Coach, one of my fellow students, from Australia, asked the question, 'how deeply do you go with the client?' The answer that came back from our teacher was, 'as far as the client wants to go'. I'd throw the same challenge out to anybody embarking upon their journey as a Transcendent Leader. You can go as deeply with this as you like. The deeper you go, the more impressive will be the manifestation.

Thus when we understand our role in creating a movement, in creating a team that acts like a neuro-network, we trigger a cycle of self-sustaining abundance in the manifest realm. But 'abundance' is a much maligned and misunderstood term, so let's just clear up a common misconception about it.

Traditional prayer asks the Creator to mercifully give us something. It is akin to religious begging. Moreover, we are never worthy ('so much as to pick up the crumbs under you table…'). Or if that doesn't work, we might try and acquire something – always through our own strength. This is old, 'dualistic' thinking, i.e. that we and the universe and God are different things. Let's not get into the theology just now, save to say that we and the universe cannot possibly be separate. As I said earlier, the very molecules in our bodies originally came from the stars, after all. So we are not separate from 'what is'. 'What is' is *us* and we are '*what is*'.

Therefore it is surely the wrong path to take to plead with something separate from ourselves to give us something, because the reality is that we are not separate from Spirit. When we plead with a distant, external God, we are starting from the assumption that the 'something' we want is 'without' us, i.e. does not currently reside within or even near to us. In Transcendent Leadership, the paradigm is completely reversed. Now, we as leaders recognise that abundance, or the thing that we want to have, is manifested endogenously, i.e. from within, rather than exogenously, or without/outside. This is because we are not separate from the universe, we are the very stuff of the universe, and after our death, we will return to the earth, to the planet.

So how is the 'stuff' of life manifest? It is manifest through becoming, through emerging. This is therefore the reason that we can talk instead about emergence, rather than about 'getting'. We are designed to grow and to manifest from the inside-out. The plant is already in the seed. It is a holon. The plant doesn't have to go out and make it happen, it just surrenders to the environment and the soil, and when the conditions and the soil are correct, then the plant emerges. Indeed, the universe in its entirety is patterned upon the paradigm of emergence.

What you need to manifest is already in you as a perfect code, and when you come into alignment with it, it will unfold in your life. Understanding this is key to flow. Misunderstand it or never get it, and your life will remain one of struggle built on a sense of lack. The harder we try to change in our own power, the more tired and drained we become. So we need to radically change course, to see the truth that is being demonstrated all around us in the natural world of which we are an intrinsic part. And this truth is that we, like the seed, are already perfectly designed to allow the abundance of the universe to manifest in us and around us and through us.

Self-driven effort when applied in a way ignorant of these truths will only serve to block the natural emergence process. When we stop, listen, surrender, contemplate and meditate, we begin to open up a space, a channel, for the emergent future to become manifest, to bubble up from a place previously unseen. Surrender therefore brings growth as we will be getting ourselves out of the way. Then the unique genius within us will begin to flow. This is the key to abundance. From nothing comes everything.

Let me now introduce a Compass Point of infinite brilliance:

Give what appears to be missing. Try it for yourself.

I was given this knowledge from a fabulous coach, a friend of mine called, Chris Neilson from San Diego. He explained that if we accept the notion that everything we need is already within us, then whatever is missing is what we are not giving. Life is not happening *to* us, it's happening *through* us. When life is flowing through us, we act as a channel for the universe. Conversely, when we try to create what we haven't got, we get burnt out. When we surrender and act as a channel, the opposite happens – we become energised, we become excited. Creativity, love, health, beauty, exuberance, all of these things flourish when we get out of the way and look to something bigger than ourselves.

My faith tradition is the Evangelical Christian Church. This book has made some leap forwards from that original position, I will admit. However, even within the evangelical church, my vicar once said, 'if you want to be filled with the Holy Spirit, first you have to step out in faith and GIVE! If you do not give, then God will have no need to be refilling you with anything!'. He was so right. Give what appears to be missing and you will begin the flow of abundance. We will explore the flow and circulation laws further below, but first, let's also get one thing straight when we talk about abundance. Wealth and abundance is never really about money *per se*.

Money in economic terms is merely a means of exchange. It's just paper, or it's just credit or it's blots of ink on a bank statement. Wealth is so much more, it's about how you feel, it's about creativity, it's about love, it's about meaning, wellbeing, security and safety and so on. It's so much more than just money. Sure it can include money, but only in terms of what you can *do* with that money. So money in these terms is really about potential, about possibility.

When I look at my own life and think about abundance, if I concentrate my gaze on money, I always think about lack – about how much more money I would really like, about how much bigger I'd like that bank balance to be. But if I turn my consciousness towards the true meaning of abundance, I think about my beautiful children, of my wife, my parents, my job, my creativity, my gifts, the beautiful place in which we live, the music that is in my life, my friends and family in South America and so on. It's never possible to think of abundance in terms of lack when I think of it in this way.

So wanting abundance is fine. It is really ok to want abundance in your life! In fact, it is brilliant that you want abundance in your life. The mere fact that you are reading this book would probably indicate that you are somebody who desires improvement, who wants to become a better leader, who wants to give of their gifts, who ultimately wants to contribute towards the evolutionary betterment of mankind on the planet today.

So think about it – would you be more effective or less effective in this mission if you had abundance or had lack in your life? Of course the answer is 'abundance' every time! So this is your inheritance, it is your 'good' it is the thing that you are – you are perfectly designed to produce the 'good' in your life that is your birthright. Abundance is already yours. So stop thinking about money, which creates a sense of lack, and think instead about true abundance.

Maybe take a few minutes and give thanks for the abundance that is in your life right here, right now in the present moment. And whilst you are in presence, it is the best possible time to step out of the way and let it naturally flow through you. It is time to allow the almost infinite potential of abundance to flow. This potential is like one of the fundamental sources of energy – potential energy. We have already said that money should not be thought about in nominal terms, i.e. notes and coins and so on. A better way to think about money in the context of abundance is as potential energy powering abundance.

So many ideas that we may have as leaders both inside and outside teams and organisations, need some kind of resource – seed money for capital or ongoing revenue. Is it not just common sense that your mission and the acceleration of projects and plans would be so much easier with more money rather than less? So throw away any guilty feelings around the accumulation of monetary wealth. If your mind is set upon your higher purpose, upon fulfilling your longest reach, then money is just another facet to the overall road map towards Transcendent Leadership, powering your journey with potential energy.

Abundance is holarchic in nature and is intimately identified with flow. The tree doesn't suddenly emerge from the seed. It is part of a cyclical process of flow. Water comes from above; nutrients come from below; both flow into the tree and the tree is thus in a process of emergence. Growth is a manifestation of the circulation of energy. In the same way as a leader, your energy with your team and in your work is fully and beautifully realised when it is channelled in a pattern of circulation from the universe. So your real wealth cannot even be seen; it is the mechanism within you that enables flow and circulation; it is simply part of your inherent nature.

When we see this truth, our eyes are opened to the beauty of abundance. When we allow the universe to flow through us and we surrender all of what we are to the evolving purpose of Spirit, then our inherent wealth produces abundance. This is nothing to be coy about or to hide. It is simply wonderful! Just think about it – without you, nothing good would flow through you, nothing would be manifest through you. With you, good things are manifest. Moreover, with you in a leadership role, abundance flows. It flows to the people that you lead, and it flows into the thing for which your team or your organisation has a purpose. This really is nothing to ever feel guilty about. So let it shine!

We must never forget therefore that our true power lies *within*. Our power does not lie with the things that we have accumulated. Accumulation brings attachment. Attachment is often to things, such as clothes, cars, homes, i.e. things that are objects. But these things are dead. A fancy car is not a living object. It is dead. But the life of abundance comes from Source, and Source is alive; abundance necessarily has a flowing, living, circulating, loving quality. So put your trust and faith in Source, not in (re)sources: Source is alive, *re*source is dead.

Let's look in more detail at flow systems and the circulation in our own internal body-mind system. Circulation is a little bit like the cycle of water on earth, which is known as the hydrologic cycle. This involves evaporation, transpiration, condensation, precipitation and runoff. It is this cycle of water that gives life to the earth. In the same way, the more circulation we can create in our own lives, the more abundance, the more energy, the more life will come through us. The same goes for the economy – it is the circular flow of money that maintains economic activity. We could have the same volume of money in an economy but if the velocity dries up, if everybody just put their money into long-term deposit accounts, then the economy would dive into recession.

The amount of abundance within our own body-spirit system is therefore simply the velocity and the volume of circulation we allow. Love, energy, manifestation, learning, growth...this is the transcendent hydrologic cycle. When we block the circulation, we get the opposite – lack of manifestation, lack of learning, lack of creativity and a moribund, stagnating life within and without.

In this respect, leadership is like being in a long-term relationship. Think about the new relationship – you give all of you to the other person – smiles, touches, flowers, your time, your humour, your attention, your love. Unfortunately, with many couples, little by little, the potential energy of these acts diminishes as boredom and patterns of behaviour creep in. It's as if somebody has switched the pump off, preventing the water from circulating in a system.

So if the additional energy of all of these little acts of love or kindness and attention are removed from the relationship, it is little wonder that circulation diminishes and love begins to die. The same goes for leadership and the abundance that can flow through us as leaders. If we fail to nurture our leadership and our relationships that stem from that position of leadership, then the energy pump is switched off, circulation (volume x velocity) diminishes and our leadership stagnates. This really should not come as a surprise to us. It's all around energy, flow and channelling of what is already within us.

How, then, do we generate more energy to produce more circulation? Firstly, do not wait for external events to begin, end or resolve.   This is an inside job, remember? It is endogenous. So the time is *now*. The person is *you*. What you need is already there, just waiting for you to claim your 'good'. It may not yet be manifest, but it's a bit like the seed asking, 'where is the fruit'? Well it's within the seed, as infinite potential. The same goes for flow which produces your abundance. You are not separate from your abundance any more than the seed is separate from the fruit. Therefore, your 'good' is already within you as a seed of potential.

You may have heard of the law of attraction. This is fundamentally flawed. It is an idea borne from duality, the notion that you are separate from the thing that you desire, therefore you somehow have to attract that thing to you. No, No, NO! If everything is within you then there's nothing to attract to you. The fruit is not attracted to the seed. The butterfly is not attracted to the chrysalis. When my children were born, love didn't come to me from anywhere else for me to give my children love – it was already inherent inside me. Indeed, not even inside me, because even this indicates duality, or separation. I am love and I circulate this love. When I circulate the love, do I lose it to another person, as if I am giving them a chunk of my chocolate bar? Of course not! Quite the opposite – the more I circulate love, the more abundantly love manifests in my life and between me and others.

In the same way, God does not *give* love – this again is dualistic thinking. The truth is that God *is* love. And if God is love, then love is God. All love is God. It simply has to be. Love is an expression of Source. It is Source. Can we directly see Source? No we cannot, but we can see expressions of Source everywhere we look. It's the paradox of 'everything and nothing'. In nothing, we find everything. Everything comes from, and emanates from nothing. That is how everything evolves, because 'what is' emanates from nothing.

We are fundamentally eternal spirit in human form; spirit having a short sojourn here on planet earth. Our ultimate mission? To contribute to the ever greater expression and expansion of that which gives rise to more 'good'. Anita Moorjani puts this so beautifully well in 'Experiencing Heaven on Earth':

> "When I was born into this world
> The only things I knew were to love, laugh, and shine my light brightly.
> Then as I grew, people told me to stop laughing.
> "Take life seriously," they said,
> "If you want to get ahead in this world."
> So I stopped laughing.
> People told me, "Be careful who you love
> If you don't want your heart broken."
> So I stopped loving.
> They said, "Don't shine your light so bright
> As it draws too much attention onto you."
> So I stopped shining
> And became small
> And withered
> And died
> Only to learn upon death
> That all that matters in life
> Is to love, laugh, and shine our light brightly!"

So this means letting the handbrake off to allow ourselves to create, to flow, to develop, to love, to give of our genius. And to do this, we simply acknowledge that everything will emanate from and through us as we surrender everything that we have to a power greater than ourselves. We get our 'gross' self (body and ego) out of the way and we become a vessel through which divine creation will manifest abundance. This is how flow, the circulation of energy, is made manifest in our lives.

When we make this shift towards understanding, it suddenly appears so very, very reasonable and true, because it is. It is like a secret that has been hiding in plain sight all along. Indeed, we can test it by applying the opposite. This might be:

- A caterpillar has to try incredibly hard and pray every night to develop into a butterfly.

- A rain drop has to work night and day with all of its might to flow into a river, to then flow into the sea, to then be evaporated, to then become part of the cloud again.

- A little girl has to try really hard to have her nails grow, her hair grow, to become taller.

- The earth has to try with all of its power and might to orbit the sun.

How ridiculous does all of this sound? Can you see now how natural it is for abundance to be the result of circulation which is the result of your simply 'being' and getting out of the way to allow this law to outwork in your life?

We as leaders have an incredible responsibility to model this to our followers. How many times have you seen a leader drained of all energy? You seem them striving with limited human energy to manage staff and resources and to keep the organisation happy. Such a leader also serves to drain their followers of energy. Conversely, leaders who understand the underpinning laws of abundance do not only allow flow through themselves, but they manifest flow throughout the entire community of followers. Everything seems just so positive, so simple and so effortless. Of course it does, because that is what abundance feels like. So whenever you feel stressed, tired, drained of energy, just become aware again of flow, get yourself out of the way, surrender and let circulation back in.

But where do we go when the circulation dries up? Turn back to the fundamental compass point – give what appears to be missing. As a leader, the first thing I do when I'm feeling out of ideas and I'm feeling flat, is to get out there and spend time with staff, with the nurses, therapists or social workers that I manage. I am not giving money away, but I am giving an even more finite resource – time and personal attention. This creates circulation, of energy, of interest, of love. Love in this instance might sound a little strong, but love is the ultimate source of abundance, it can come from listening, from connecting, from taking a deep and honest interest in another person.

Think for yourself the things that you give as a leader which act as a pump for the circuit. Write them down, maybe in the notes section on your mobile device. Go to this when you intuitively feel that the circuit needs more flow, more power.

You also need to retain and maintain this powerful circulation and this is where the following chapter on rest comes in. If all you do is energetically pump, pump, pump in your own power, then you will soon deplete yourself of energy. Even when we are getting out of the way and allowing source to manifest through us, the very act of creativity, of being a servant to Source, can be draining.

Likewise with your team, there are times to give, and there are times to retreat and rest a little. The times that seem like 'downtime' really are not that. Downtime is a necessary part of circulation. It adds to the sustenance of the system. Again thinking of the tree, winter is a time when the tree seemingly lies dormant; it is the time when the dormouse hibernates. Seemingly nothing is happening, but this time when nothing happens lays the foundation for the time when everything happens, and infinite potential is realised. Think also about the cycle of your breath. Without breathing out, you can never breathe in. Breathing out releases the space for the next breath. Rest, or downtime releases the space and energy for the next wave of activity in a team.

Those people you know who are relentlessly energetic, who appear to have it all – money, happy family, four hours' sleep a night, exotic travel, promotion after promotion – they are like the person who never breathes out. It might look good in the moment, but at some time, they will go bang!

At this point, it's also worth a reminder about how resistance might serve to impede your manifestation practice. The power and negative charge of resistance and self-sabotage are not to be under-estimated. Let's begin with who or what is doing the resisting. Just reflect for a moment - when you talk about the 'I', for example, 'I want to be the best leader that I can possibly be', you have to question, 'who is this, 'I'?

There is the fundamental 'you', the highest form of consciousness that is the subjective seer of everything else. This is the part of you often described as the soul, the 'real you'. Beneath this level of ultimate consciousness, there is no single 'I'. The person that is you underneath this level isn't just one person, rather, it is like a multitude of chattering people on the top deck of a bus. One wants to do something, the other one resists and even actively sabotages. For example, you realise that summer is on the way and you want to look better in your swimwear. So one of the people on the top deck of the bus decides to go on a diet. And a lot of the time, they're doing pretty well. But then you get home from work with the munchies. So another one of the people goes searching in the fridge, resisting the new goal. Yet another person on the bus sabotages, by buying a stack of Pringles in the supermarket, ready for the next munchies moment.

The same can apply with Transcendent Leadership. It can sometimes be so easy just to return to the safe territory of the transactional level: conscious-less setting of agendas, churning through e-mails, schlepping along to meetings. Therefore if you want to get anything out of this book at all, if you have found inspiration in it, if there's one part of you on top of that bus that says, *'Yes! I'm going to let this change my life, I'm going to rocket on up to cruising altitude and transcend all previous levels of leadership practice – bring it on!'*, then read this next paragraph very, very carefully.

This does not just happen automatically. You have to very consciously decide to do this and also be very conscious of overcoming resistance and self-sabotage. One of my favourite theories, 'Spiral Dynamics', closely related to Integral Theory which I have already mentioned, talks about lines of intelligence, or development.

The lines include cognitive, ethical, aesthetic, inter-personal, intra-personal, spiritual, kinaesthetic, affective, musical, spatial, logical-mathematical, linguistic, karmic and so on. For example, one could be brilliant in the spatial-kinaesthetic arena (such as sports professionals), but absolutely useless when it comes to mathematics. One of the most important of the intelligences is that of 'will-power', for it is this intelligence that knits the development of all of the other lines of intelligence together. Willpower often involves a conscious, voluntary and intentional 'push' on our part. Without the intentionality, you have only natural conditioning to fall back on. A vast swathe of the population operates seemingly without will power encroaching in any meaningful way on their lives. They are slaves to the fridge and the sofa.

There are times that we have to push, really, really hard. There are times, however, when we need not to push so hard, when we are called upon to use more subtle techniques. You need to attune your consciousness to discriminate between when to push to create momentum, and when you need to simply set an intention and then stand aside. An example of the latter is when you are inviting the universe into a situation that is not entirely in your control in terms of outcomes. In those moments, invite, set your intention and then get out of the way, don't push. This is because much of the time, when you push, it's not a push, it's actually just another form of resistance.

It's naturally difficult for those of us who have been taught that we have to try extremely hard, to the end of our powers, to make a superhuman effort. This is fine at Levels One and Two but at Level Three, we are operating not in our own power but in oneness with the power of the cosmos. It's an order of magnitude different.

Thus resistance can occur in a negative way – we sabotage the very thing that we are striving for, It can also occur in a positive way – by pushing too hard in our own power when we ought to be letting go of our own power and surrendering the outcome to the great power of universal consciousness. Learning when to push and when to surrender is something that can only come about through experience. However, as a guide, if you've been pushing hard and things aren't manifesting, that's usually a signal to slide to the other side of the polarity and to practise surrender.

The good news is that like other lines of intelligence, willpower and knowing when to let go can be practised and moulded into a habit - something that becomes a natural part of your every day existence. Consciousness is the key to this. You can set daily diary reminders for, say, mid-morning, or for when you arrive at work. They could be around pre-set practices, or even just a general reminder – something like, 'be aware', 'breathe', 'cruising altitude', 'transcend the mundane today'. Whatever works for you.

We are entering new territory here, and our ancient, reptilian brain wants to keep us in the safe zone. Beware of this - nothing incredible, game-changing or disruptive happens in the safe-zone! We were not put onto this planet to operate in the safe zone. If you are finding the shift difficult, search within yourself to see where the sticking point is. It is often something that we are trying desperately to hold on to, in areas of our life where we are not willing to give up, to surrender to the power bigger than us. If you want to hold onto some elements then that's your call, but it's this barrier of self-control, of egoic mind, that we have to transcend to rise up to Third Level.

Co-creation with Spirit can only happen if surrender is present. The problem is that pre-surrender, Second Stage, Conscious Control, can feel so empowering. Putting yourself in what seems like the driving seat can be such a rush. Of course it is – it's exactly what the ego craves. However, once you have experienced the sunny uplands of conscious surrender, there really is no turning back. In conscious surrender, there's an even greater rush, but it's not a rush of control, rather it's a rush of *flow*.

It reminds me of when I was training as a scuba diver. Compressed air at depth, at pressure contains an enormous volume of air. If you take it to a lower pressure environment, it expands. One of the exercises you have to practice when training to be a scuba diver is an emergency ascent, as if your air supply has failed. Therefore, you take a breath of air at around 10 metres in depth, then you ascend at the same rate as the bubbles around you. This takes some time, and for the duration, you are not allowed to take another breath of air. All of which would be impossible on the surface as the ascent time is longer than you can normally hold your breath for. However, as you rise from depth, the air in your lungs expands. If you hold your breath, you will effectively explode such is the volume of air inside you. One breath of air at ten metres is the same amount of air that is contained in a wardrobe at the surface!

So as you ascend, you have to keep the airway open to avoid a human explosion. You do this by looking up to the surface and humming. As you do this, the air in your lungs expands and there's only one way out – through your throat and out of your mouth. It's one of the strangest feelings you can experience, an incredible rush of air coming seemingly from nowhere, shooting out of your mouth. At no time do you feel out of breath, even though the ascent takes one to two minutes. The feeling of power is awesome, even though you are not controlling it, or pushing it.

Such is the feeling when Spirit takes hold of your leadership practice, at Third Level. Its power is immense; there's an incredible feeling of flow; it feels as if it is not coming from you but that it is flowing *through* you. As for me, I have to say my ego does rather enjoy feeling as if it is in the driving seat when I'm at Second Stage. I often like the feeling that I am taking control and pushing hard. But it pales into insignificance compared to the riches I know are in store for me at Third Level. I have been practising the latter for so long that I personally need little in terms of willpower to maintain my practice, just a gentle nudge from time to time when I feel myself falling back into unconscious Second Level habits.

Finally, let me just re-emphasise the biggest misconception of all about surrender. It is absolutely not about giving up. It has nothing to do with the negative, weak, traditional meaning of the word. It's not about waving the white flag! Divine surrender has an entirely different charge at a fundamental level. At the human level, the ego resists surrender with everything that it has. This is because it naturally feels as if we are losing something. The very act of letting go is antithetical to the ego. So let's not pretend for a minute that the act of surrender does not feel like a loss to self, indeed, sometimes even as a loss *of* self.

We have such an attachment to the thing that our small mind thinks is the real 'us', our bodies, our history, our mind, our thoughts, our gifts and so on. To surrender a belief for instance, can feel as if we are wrenching something away from us. So try this as a practice:

Surrender everything that you think that you know. Surrender everything that you don't yet know. Write down on a piece of paper the things that you are attached to, be they physical items or beliefs or prejudices. Then write down things that are on the edge of attachment and knowledge for you, things that you partially identify with. Then draw a box shape with nothing in it. This represents everything that you don't yet know. This is important, because in this exercise you can surrender the past, the now and the future all at once.

Now say that you surrender these things. You give them up. You are surrendering your small self, your humanness. Take a moment to really let this sink in. Now turn the paper over.

Open up to the knowing that goes beyond your mind. Look at the blank sheet of paper before you. It has no writing on it as yet. This seeming blank piece of paper before you isn't in fact blank at all as it is representative of everything. Imagine that it is a piece of paper upon which is actually written *everything*. It is the field of infinite possibility upon which the divine dances.

I want you now to become one with the divine in your walk upon this planet by opening up to your divinity.

Open yourself up to the field of infinite possibility that the blank sheet of paper represents. This is a sacred act of owning and embodying your divinity. You are bringing it from the third person, the 'other', or God if you like, and bringing it into alignment with the first person, i.e. what you call 'I'. You are then passing through the stage of alignment and making the most radical shift of all as you bring it right into you. You become one with this thing. You do not only align with it, you ARE it. You have surrendered the small self and welcomed in and become one with the divinity that is your *big self*, your *real self*.

In this way, you are allowing your own divinity to fully immerse within the body. It's essentially a divinity embodiment practice in which you allow the divine to work within you at a soul level and to use you as a human outworking of the intentions of God on this planet. That's what Third Level is all about. You have made the shift from being a body controlled by small-mind, towards being an entire being given over to the divine! There cannot be many more powerful concepts than that in the field of leadership, indeed, humanity.

To summarise: We let go of our humanness, then we embody our divinity and then we return to embodying our humanness. Those familiar with the theory of soft systems analysis will recognise this. In this theory, in order to move forwards, we take a real life problem, we then shift into theoretical and conceptual frameworks to analyse the problem and identify a solution. We finally return back to the real world to embed the theoretical solution back into the world of form.

Here, we do much the same work, just at the level of humanity and spirit. We start with our embodied humanity. We work at the human level on taking Conscious Control at the egoic level (Level Two); we then shift into the world of Spirit through an act of conscious surrender, where we let go of the ego self; and finally we implant the new divine body and spirit-level understanding back into our humanity and into our field of leadership.

We are left with a communion between humanity and divinity. This then becomes the tap which switches on the flow. This is the ultimate marriage of form and the formless. It is a wonderful example of the both/and universe that we inhabit. We are neither pure humanity struggling with human emotions and ego; neither are we a pure spiritual being, sat in the apocryphal cave meditating all day long. We can be both fully human and fully divine at one and the same time. Allowing the divine into our mission truly shifts us to a new level that has absolutely nothing to do with the world that we used to know.

What we have done is to turn over the page containing our egoic desires, the things that we think we need in our life; the things that we think that we want. We are letting all of this go. When we turn the page over and offer up a blank page for Spirit to work upon, this will allow what is really destined for our life to come in. It's as if we have taken away the foundations of our life, built by us, the hand of a human, and replaced them with a foundation made of Spirit.

Imagine that our life is made up of bricks or building blocks. Each of those blocks is an element of our life. It might be a thing like a person, a loved one, or it might be an object, such as a TV or a car or a handbag. It could even be a non-physical thing such as a thought or a self-belief.

The things that are causing us pain that produce resistance can be identified as bricks in a wall. When I am coaching somebody, I will often listen to them for up to 15 minutes telling me their story. I am not particularly interested in the actual narrative of the story itself, unlike the person themselves who is normally entirely absorbed and identified with the story. It's not that I am uninterested in the person. On the contrary, because I am so interested in the person, I try to see the person hidden behind the narrative. What I am entirely focussed on, what I am looking out for, are the bricks in the wall as each of these bricks represents a symptom or a cause of the suffering within the person.

My task through understanding and intuition is to spot which of the bricks is the symptom and which is the cause. The cause is almost always an underlying (often hidden) belief that does not serve that person's higher good. An example would be if somebody were to be blindly going for promotion constantly, trying to prove themselves. This 'symptom brick' might be taking a toll on their life and on their relationships. An underlying belief, on another brick as it were might be, 'I'm not good enough'. Thus the striving for promotion is linked with the latter belief. Thus the 'not good enough' would be a 'symptom brick'.

Another symptom might be lack of sleep and over-activity. The underlying belief behind this could be, 'there is not enough time'. Thus the symptom is insomnia, the cause is 'there's not enough time'.

Often there are a whole host of symptom bricks, potentially hundreds of them in fact. When one starts to look at the underlying causal bricks, these essentially underpin the symptoms. Hence I see them as the foundations, or foundational bricks. I then map out all of the foundational/causal bricks and the symptom bricks. In so doing, I map out which one of the foundational bricks sit under each of the symptom bricks. Each time I do this, it's astonishing how vanishingly few foundation bricks there actually are.

Typically, they consist of the two given above, as well as, 'nobody loves me', 'nobody listens to me', 'there's never enough money' and just a handful more. They are nearly exclusively connected with a sense of 'lack'.

If you're struggling to overcome your innate resistance to surrender, try this practice for yourself and seek the foundational bricks that underlie this resistance.

We can play this game on an organisational level as well. I've mentioned already that I was once Head of Performance and Planning for a large mental health organisation in London. We were located in an area of London next to the world renowned Maudsley Hospital, and we felt very much like its poor relation. I was fortunate to work alongside some brilliant minds. A close colleague of mine was the Head of Service Improvement. He once said to me, 'Richard, I'm going to bring you over from the dark side!'. Now being a nice kind of chap, this rather shocked me.

However, it was one of the most positively charged shocks I've ever had. He was a bright and experienced man, who went on to become a Deputy CEO of another large London Mental Health organisation. He and I became a formidable team, achieving performance gains through facilitating service improvement, rather than the usual techniques of setting unachievable targets, terrorising managers and staff and smothering them with threats.

I'm always on the look out for simplicity and effective solutions. And I stumbled upon one whilst counting the targets we were supposed to hit. We worked in an immensely complex world. Over 40 different regulators, Quangos and inspectors could walk through the doors of our Head Quarters for one reason or another. So I counted the targets associated with each one. And I counted. And I counted. I stopped when I got bored at around 650.

I sat at the board table one afternoon and wrote as many as I could on sticky notes. After an hour or so, the board table was absolutely covered with them. So I started putting them into order and eventually they looked like the bricks of a wall, as with the coaching technique outlined above. And I then decided to look at patterns. When I recognised that I was actually looking at a wall of bricks, I wondered what the foundation bricks were. It turned out that there weren't many. I counted six. All six were also targets in and of themselves.

The magic of the six, however, is that they each had scores and scores of other targets that sat on top of them, that were linked to them. An example was sickness. At the time, the rate of absence in the health service nationally was running at about 5 percent. Industry was around half that level. Therefore it became a national priority to reduce the level of sickness (along with the hundreds of other targets!).

However, the obvious conclusion that came to me is that sickness is also linked with good finances (decrease sickness rates, you decrease spend on agency workers), productivity, morale, patient quality, reduction in numbers of complaints and so on. So I realized that if we solved these six foundational bricks, everything else would fall into place.

I remember yanking the CEO out of his office and into the board room to show him this map. When I told him that if we sorted out just six key targets, we'd solve the lot of them, his eyes lit up. So that's what we did. And later that year, when the two key performance ratings for all mental health organisations in the country were announced, we topped the league table, much to the chagrin of the famous Maudsley Hospital next door!

Try doing the same for all of the targets in your organisation. Can you identify foundational bricks that hold up everything you are attempting to do? If you can, you will be able to pay attention and manage just a fraction of the things that you previously had to because everything else will fall into place.

Turning away from things that trouble us or strategic targets, we can also turn the exercise on its head and do the same for all of the positive things in our life. Take all of the things that you are grateful for, write them down on small pieces of paper or sticky notes. Then arrange them in a brick-like wall. Put the foundation bricks at the bottom and draw relationships between them.

When I do this exercise, the foundation bricks are things like: my parents, my wife, my children, my friends, my education, my health, my job, my curiosity, my passions, connecting with my higher self; with God. Upon these foundations everything else sits. Try it for yourself and see what the foundational bricks are. Then give thanks for them, plus all the bricks above them. Nurture and care for the foundational bricks and you will see a great flourishing of abundance in all of the areas of your life that are connected with them.

So where does this sit with respect to Transcendent Leadership? Well, this foundational/symptom brick practice is a great technique at the cusp of Second and Third Levels for you to adopt into whatever organisation you work in. The change, however, comes when we open the exercise up to the infinite realm. Doing this brings in resonance from the transcendent. When we do this, the foundation stones of our life are no longer our own resource, desires, qualities and so on. Now they radically shift into the divine realm.

The foundation that underlies everything is instead like a brilliant white light. It's filled with Spirit. Our foundation is our new divine embodiment. Our ego, our small mind falls away. Divinity flows through us. We move from the finite to the infinite. There is a sense of oneness. Oneness within ourselves – the spirit, mind and body become one thing; oneness with all of humanity; oneness with all of nature. And yes, oneness as a leader with those that we lead, oneness of the corporate body because we now see the team that we lead as being itself connected with the light of the divine.

"The total number of minds in the universe is one. In fact, consciousness is a singularity phasing within all beings"

Dr Erwin Schrödinger

To summarise, whether we are analysing our resistance to surrender or our strategic aims and organisational goals, we can always find half a dozen foundational building blocks to each of these areas by analysing the underlying structures upon which everything else rests. And each of these in turn sits upon the whole light of spirit. It's spirit that connects everything. It's not all the same thing objectively, but subjectively at the level of the numinous, it is all one. Our team, our purpose, our spirit - it is one united singularity.

As I write these words, in a moment of divine synchronicity, I am playing a Johnny Cash playlist, and the perfect lyrics to illustrate that last point are resonating around my room:

> "One love,
> One blood,
> One life,
> You've got to do what you should
> One life with each other
> Sister
> Brothers
> One life but we're not the same
> We get to carry each other
> Carry each other
> One..."
>
> *Original song by U2*

We are now in a position to summarise the seventh dimension of Transcendent Leadership: When you co-create with Spirit, abundance arises through flow. Space arises for brilliant people to be brilliant, and the team develops its own learning and growth through neuroplasticity. Through this, goals are made manifest.

Summary of Practices and Reflections in this dimension:

- Light Workers   179

- Prosperity Manifestation   184

- Manifest Brilliance   188

- Abundance   197-198

- Flow and Circulation   199-201

- When to Push, When to Surrender   208

- Surrender the Ego and Align with Divinity   212

- Foundational and Symptomatic Bricks   214-218

Chapter 8

The Eighth Dimension: Resting

The Mind-Spirit Energy Cycle

Finally we come metaphorically to the end of the day. Much of this book has been around action, around doing – manifesting, organising, transmitting and so on. But you can only do this if you have something left in the locker. The Transcendent Leader needs to be at ease with him or herself. No great leader can perform or even open to be a channel if they are not fundamentally 'ok', and I would argue that nobody can be truly 'ok' if they are not at ease and able to truly rest on a frequent basis.

The Transcendent Leader is deeply connected to the stillness of eternity. Connecting with the silence within, the Transcendent Leader finds the still point around which the business of the world pivots. This eternal singularity serves as a place of refuge and of retreat. It's the place where we commune with the divine, a place of infinite energy and renewal.

I am blessed in my day job of having a phenomenal team around me. There's a degree of luck involved in having arrived in such a position, but this luck has been nurtured through much thought and design. Last year, I put Sarah, one of my managers, forward for a national award, and she won it, to become Team Manager of the Year for England and Wales - quite an accolade. One of the spin-offs of being awarded this prize is that the following year, you get to sit on the judging panel. Thus she went home one night with the long-list of 26 people, one of whose references she read out to me the next morning. This person's manager put them forward for the award, saying that they were the proverbial 110% committed to the role. In fact, so committed were they that they were always the first to arrive in the morning at 7:00 am; they were also the last to leave at 7:30 pm in the evening. They did this every single day of the week, and often even at weekends. They volunteered for anything going.

We were reflecting together on this application for a prize, and Sarah said, 'what kind of a leader is this?!', she must be absolutely burnt out. Burnt out leaders are devoid of energy. They often look pale, sick and haggard. It is not pleasant to work for a leader like this. Furthermore, being such a leader cannot be any fun either. There can be no possibility of having any mental or physical energy spare to be able to perform the other actions necessary to Transcendent Leadership that we have as chapter headings of this book. There can be little or no knowing, seeing, being, aligning, connecting and certainly no creating. And what of those powerful coaching questions I have mentioned – how can such a person be able to realise their deepest longing; achieve their highest reach; be the best version of themselves? None of these things is possible if the tank is empty.

This is so very far from unusual, however. So many leaders are stressed, angry, unsettled, trapped in an endless cycle of thinking, doing, thinking, doing. Such is their heightened state of arousal that their body is wracked with overdoses of the stress hormones – adrenaline, cortisol and norepinephrine. If you have ever worked for a leader in this cycle, you will know that it is almost impossible for them not to transmit this to you and everybody else in the team.

Thus it is of vital importance that within the daily routine of the Third Level leader, there is time and space to switch the leadership mind-body system off; to enter the stillness.

This has to start with exercises to still the mind. This can be so difficult for many high achievers. We have spoken earlier in the book about the need for passion, for drive, for the knowledge that you are placed upon this planet to exercise your unique genius. For many such people, they struggle to seemingly abandon this passion in the act of rest. For them, the act of abandonment, of switching down the thought-action cycle is to deny the passion that drives them. For them, their mind is attached to the drive, the power, the doing, the people, the results.

You may yourself identify with these sentiments. There are probably vanishingly few people that are attracted to a book entitled, 'Transcendent Leadership' who do not aspire to the very apogee of leadership practice. Thus for many, I will have to be extremely convincing to establish in their minds the central importance of pressing the standby or even the shut down button on a daily basis.

The most cogent argument is to be found in the world of physical training. Take weight training for instance. Successful athletes recognise the dangers of over-training. When lifting weights, your body is actually breaking down muscle. It is ripping the muscle fibres. When you take in nutrition and you rest, the muscle is built back up. The body repairs itself; it strengthens itself in-between workouts. Recovery and rest enables the body to repair damaged tissues and to reverse the depletion of energy stores (glycogen in the muscles) that takes place during workouts.

In 2013, Dr Maiken Nedergaard, a neurologist at the University of Rochester in New York, published an article in the journal, 'Science' which described sleep as a waste removal system for the brain. The study showed that brain cells shrink during sleep to open up gaps between neurons and allow fluid to wash the brain clean. Dr Nedergaard said, 'The brain only has limited energy at its disposal and it appears that it must choose between two different functional states – awake and aware or asleep and cleaning up…you can think of it like having a house party. You can either entertain the guests or clean up the house, but you can't really do both at the same time.'

In this way, sleep clears toxic proteins known as beta-amyloid, from the brain which if left un-cleansed, may lead to various forms of dementia. Those leaders who practice macho sleep-deprivation, believing it to be something for the weak and for those less driven than themselves, are storing up problems both in the present and in later life. Both Margaret Thatcher and Ronald Reagan were very vocal about sleeping only four to five hours per night. Perhaps unsurprisingly, both went on to develop dementia.

Maybe think about keeping a sleep diary for a month. Write down, too, how energised you feel the next day. Do you see a correlation? Do you find that by measuring your sleep you develop better sleep hygiene?

So sleep in and of itself is vitally important. But so, too is rest in general, as is solitude. The leader can only lead in relationship to other people. A solitary actor is only the leader of him or herself after all, thus the leader is a person who often lacks solitude. As a result, energy levels can be depleted via a work-life that is very crowded.

When I worked in London, I worked for a manager who was a staggeringly intelligent woman and a great leader. Rather surprisingly, she once admitted to being an extreme introvert. I had never seen her as such, given the amount of speaking events and meetings that she attended. However, being an introvert, she recharged her batteries by being alone. She once confided in me that as soon as she arrived home on a Friday night, her favourite weekend consisted of closing the front door and only opening it again come Monday morning.

Research suggests that most CEOs are in fact introverts. The stereotype of the CEO is the heroic leader; the person that oozes charisma, who fills the room with their sparkling presence; the person who takes control and who charges from the front. The reality is different. Whilst around 40% of the population describes themselves as being introvert, around 70% of CEOs do so. Why does this make them so effective? CEOs have to be able to read and absorb a lot of information – Board reports, emails and research papers. This involves a lot of introverted activity.

Even if you are not an introvert, the practice of solitude acts much like sleep does in the brain, washing clean the system. How much of the time do we carry around with us unresolved problems from the day? How often are we still working in our minds when we have returned from work? We might be showering, putting the kids to bed, cooking, watching TV, but in our minds we are worrying, planning, analysing, sifting, feeling anger, judging colleagues, holding resentment about the boss. Sleep, solitude, meditation, or simply having fun with friends and family is a wonderful antidote to these things. We absolutely must let go and wash the system clean. Every day.

There is a wonderful Zen Buddhist parable that illustrates this lesson wonderfully:

"Two monks (one old and one young) were travelling from one monastery to another. They were celibate monks, not even allowed to direct their gaze at women. After a long walk, they came to a river, which they had to cross. The river was flooded and there was no way that they would get across without getting wet. One lady was also at the banks of river, wanting to cross; she was weeping because she was afraid to cross on her own.

The Monks decided to cross the river by walking through the relatively shallow part of the river. Since the lady also needed to get to the other bank, the older monk, without much ado, carried her on his shoulders, and soon they reached the other bank, where he set her down. The lady went her way and the two monks continued their walk in silence. The other monk was really upset, finding the other monk's act disturbing. As per their injunctions, they were not allowed to look at the woman, let alone touch a woman, and yet the other monk carried her on his shoulders and all the way across the river!

After a few hours the confused monk couldn't stand the thought of what had happened which kept filling his mind, and so he began to berate the other monk, "We are not allowed to look at other women, not touch them, but you carried that woman."

'Which woman?' replied the older monk.
"The woman you carried on your shoulders across the river!"
The other monk paused and with a smile on his lips he said, 'I put her down when I crossed the river, are you still carrying her?'"

Quoted from patrickwanis.com

Rest and ease establishes flow. It is the pump behind the system. It establishes balance between the giving and the receiving; it promulgates circulation; it establishes a connection between heaven and earth, transmitted through you. Without the recycling of energy, you will never be able to reach the greatest good, the greatest depths of your ability as a leader, to do what you are here to do; to fulfil your mission and purpose. I have talked in previous chapters about energy and the flow of energy within your system. Clean, fresh energy allows clear seeing for the Transcendent Leader. It is so at odds with the embattled, busy, frantic and muddled energy of many leaders trapped in the lower levels of leadership.

I have mentioned the programs that inhabit our minds; that we are conditioned to obey these programs that have become embedded and run our thoughts and dictate our actions. One of the most common programs that I have observed to be loaded into the minds of leaders is that of 'busyness', the belief that as a leader, we simply must fill every day with corybantic activity, and that we must moreover, *be seen* to be filling every waking minute with some kind of a deranged frenzy.

Such leaders never emerge from the pit. I know several; they wear their activity as a mark of heroism. The first thing that they will tell you is how busy it is – 'it's just crazy out there, man!' I am left singularly unimpressed. Here are people paid to be leaders who are acting out a fantasy of the leader they are pre-programed to believe is the intrepid, energetic, valiant person that they have to be. It is a pathetic fantasy world.

If you can identify in any way with this description, then STOP! Stop right now. Relax! You are killing yourself and everybody else around you! The leaders that this world demands at this time are those that operate at Third Level. These are the real heroes of today's world. Only in transcending the false programing of this world can you rise above the mire of frenetic busyness and truly lead your organisation towards brilliance. But you have to stop and discard the ego-led specious nonsense and bombast of the stressed-out busy leader that you might have become.

So prioritise. Write a list of all of the things that you're working on at the present time. Mark them 1 to 10 in terms of their importance to your overall mission. Rank them. Then be ruthless in culling the lowest scoring objectives. Don't let them creep back into your diary. If they really must be done but they're not urgent, then time-table them in for later in the year. Learn to devote your precious time only to the mission-critical objectives.

At the same time, you also have to learn to be selfish! I call it, 'appropriate selfishness'. This is where you throw off the shackles of having to demonstrate overt external activity and instead from time to time, be selfish with your time. Do it appropriately, that is, know that the time that you spend away from others replenishing your energy and building up knowledge, will create the environment within yourself that can then see you emerging as somebody better able to serve the greater good of the team.

I once managed a clinical psychologist, a great man of immense wisdom, insight and humour. He was a man that I liked to spend time with. He was the man with whom I first coined the phrase, 'appropriate selfishness'. He used to spend one day per month simply reading. This is a habit that I adopted some twenty years ago and which I practice to this day. So many useful articles, academic papers and strategic documents come my way and ordinarily there is little or no chance that I can get to read them. So I put them in a tray, and once a month I mark a meeting in my diary, usually on a Friday afternoon, when things are calming down a little, and I take the pile of reading and spend three or four hours in my home study simply reading. And thinking. It's selfish (at least in the sense that I am by myself) and it is highly appropriate. I'd encourage you to try it for yourself.

How else then, do you break the spell? To make that shift from business and being constantly surrounded by people, meetings and activity, and learn to slow down, to widen the vision? A fabulous short cut to making the shift can be found in the writings of Dr Les Fehmi PhD. He and Jim Robbins wrote a seminal book, 'The Open Focus Brain'. There are many approaches to relaxation, some of which I have documented in my book, 'Mind-Spirit Detox'. The Open Focus Brain technique, however, is a great one to use within corporate and non-spiritual environments because whilst it is a great adjunct to spiritual meditative practices as it can also be used in an entirely secular way. It is a great shortcut to brain entrainment and the ability to train the brain to switch to different wavelengths. Understanding brain function is key to consciously operating at Third Level. (You can find a video review I recorded of The Open Focus Brain here: https://www.youtube.com/watch?v=DZtQZpjKeUI)

The brain is an electrochemical organ. The electrical activity emanating from the brain can be seen as brainwaves. These are produced by synchronised electrical pulses when neurons communicate with each other. There are five main types:

Gamma: These are the fastest brainwaves, and are associated with the highest state of focus and peak concentration. These occur between 38 and 42 Hz.

Beta: This occurs between 14 and 30 Hz and is associated with being highly alert and focused. If you are concentrating and working on something, but not at peak arousal, you will be in this state. It occurs for instance, if you are working on a spreadsheet or answering e-mails, or if you are engaged in decision making or judgement and choices. Ideas, thoughts and solutions will be pinging around your brain. It is associated with our normal waking state of consciousness.

Alpha: If you are fully aware of being aware, and are in a state of presence, or maybe you are in a light meditative state, then your brain will be in Alpha. It occurs between 8 and 12 Hz and is associated with relaxation, creativity and visualisation. This is why it is almost impossible to be highly creative whilst sitting at your desk or around the Board table.

Theta: These brainwaves occur between 3 and 8 Hz, so their amplitude is greater, with a slower frequency. In this state, tasks become so automated that you can mentally disengage from them. Thoughts are free-flow and imagination soars; it is a very positive state to be in mentally. You enter theta when drifting off to sleep. Just think how many beautiful and creative thoughts come to you just before you drift off to sleep. Many musicians find beautiful and extraordinary melodies and songs coming to them in this state. Intuition is heightened. In theta, our senses are drawn away from the external world; as such, theta is associated with deep meditation.

Delta: The brainwaves in delta are of greatest amplitude and slowest frequency. They occur between 0 to 4 Hz. Delta is associated with detached awareness, sleep and healing. Deep dreamless sleep occurs in delta. It is highly restorative.

Think about your typical day at work. In everyday life, we often focus very narrowly on specific objects whether they be physical things or the objects of thought. We seldom widen our field of vision. As we can see from the descriptions above, when we are concentrating on a specific thing, and we are in a conscious, waking state, our brains are in Beta wavelengths. This is a very short wavelength mode of brain operation. If you live constantly in this mode of focused concentration for too long, you may end up with flight/fright/freeze syndrome. This is a principle cause of stress – being in Beta too frequently. This is one reason why teachers get easily burnt out. If you're working at a desk, you are able to slip into Alpha from time to time, to pause, to look out of the window, or 'zone out'. If you are in front of a classroom of 30 children for hour after hour, your brain cannot make that shift out of Beta, which is extremely tiring and debilitating.

The children being taught, however, who have yet to learn poor patterns of thought or who are able to zone out, don't have this problem. They play, they daydream, they live in a little fantasy world. Their brain dips frequently into Alpha, Delta and Theta. Levels of stress are vastly reduced.

For his PhD thesis, Les Fehmi worked with hundreds of students and volunteers to figure out how to most rapidly shift the brain into the more diffuse focus of theta and delta. He wired volunteers up to brain wave monitors and asked them to undertake many different exercises to see which was most effective and rapid.

Fehmi first tried the traditional technique of Zen Buddhism, i.e. sitting looking at a blank wall with back upright, trying to think of nothing, that of training yourself to lose thought. For many people, this is intensely difficult. For me, it is like telling you not to think about pink elephants for the next five minutes. It becomes like mental torture.

My personal approach to things is rather like Fehmi's – I like to always think hard about the fastest way of achieving the best results. When I was at university, I put as much effort into analysing patterns of past questions and figuring out how best to use my brain's resources of recollection, as I did actually studying. Likewise with leadership. There's always a hard way and an easy way. This book is my attempt to gift people the shortest possible route to Third Level Leadership. I have been learning this for the best part of twenty years. If there are multiple ways to achieve the same results, I have been presenting you with the shortest route.

Dr Fehmi did likewise. From all of the techniques he tested, the open focus techniques were by far the most effective and rapid. We humans like to focus on *things*. That's just what we do as people – it's the way our brains are wired, at least in the west. That's why focusing on *nothing*, which is what some meditative practices call for, can be so difficult to many people. The genius of Fehmi's technique is that it follows the path of maximum simplicity and maximum results. Thus is requires focusing of the mind. However, instead of focusing on *something*, it requires us to focus on *nothing*. So you focus on space; you focus on distance between objects; you focus on space within a room. It is staggering just how effective this simple technique is.

I knew that open focus would open my brain to creativity, to other modes of being, that I would be able to see and hear things better; to intuit better; to lock into the present moment more effectively. Even so, I was astonished at my experience of the jump into open focus when I began following Fehmi's instructions.

I especially recall doing this practice with my friend, Remko, one time when we were leading some seminars in Europe. We were stood outside and the view was of people, grassland, trees, forest and some coloured sails strung from the trees. Instead of focusing on the forest in the distance, we focused on the space between us and the forest. Instead of focusing on the trees, we focused on the space between the branches. There was a shed in the middle distance. We focused on the space between the uprights of wood holding up the veranda.

After doing the exercise, we were both standing together really quite transfixed and awestruck at how our perception had shifted. Everything seemed more three dimensional; colours were more vibrant, the people shone with pellucid energy. Even our hearing seemed more acute. It was really quite remarkable. The rest of the day felt as if energy flowed right through me, as if I had become translucent and receptive. Through Open Focus, we were able to shift into Alpha and Theta whilst in an awakened state and by so doing, allow other frequencies to enter into us for the rest of the day.

So be aware of your brain and what state it is in, both when resting and when engaged in activity. Then go on to explore Open Focus and other 'brain hacks' in order that you can be more in control of the power of your mind, rather than living your life in servitude of it.

Let me really emphasise at this stage that the point of Transcendent Leadership is to open a world of radical transformation to unlock the most highly evolved levels of leadership available to us on the planet today. It is not to simply live life in blissed-out spaciousness. That is why this dimension of Third Level leadership – that of rest, is merely one of the eight dimensions. It needs to come into balance with all other seven dimensions.

Moreover, do not forget that Level Three is built upon and necessitates the presence of the other two levels. None of what I have taught in this book negates the need for activities at Level One – policy formation and implementation, planning, research, accounting, marketing, payments, personnel processes, objective setting, risk management, good governance, horizon-scanning, strategic relationships, the use of capital, applying key performance indicators, establishing lean processes etc. etc. All of these are vital components of an efficient and thriving organisation. Descriptions of why, how, when, and where to apply these Level One and Two techniques can be found throughout management and leadership literature, so I haven't attempted to reproduce much if any of that here.

Third Level insight and understanding, moreover, is like an underpinning operating system that will truly take you, your team and your organisation to the next dimension of possibility. Organisations and the leaders and managers within them can often become numbed to the overall mission of the organisation and their role within it. The daily drudge of routine and Level One activity can make one blasé. When we shift into a profound understanding of our own radiance and our deepest purpose, we are no longer caught up in the institutionalised rituals of our organisation. Instead, we remember the primary objective of life which is to connect with our divine genius and then to give it away. When we become fully conscious of our highest purpose as a leader, we radiate blessing and transmit divine possibility into those around us.

****

As we reach the end of the book, let me take the opportunity to recap. There are eight dimensions to unlocking Transcendent Leadership. The first four are foundational dimensions. These form the basic building blocks of fundamental knowledge that you need in order to make the shift to Level Three – knowing, seeing, being and aligning. Once in place, you only need to shift your awareness back to them from time to time. They are effectively breakthroughs in understanding of and locating of self. A breakthrough is a breakthrough – you don't keep having to do it, merely remind yourself of it when occasion dictates.

The final half of the book, the last four dimensions, are cyclical in nature – connecting, creating, doing and resting. These four dimensions never end. They are all part of the cycle of leadership, a flow of endless circularity akin to the ebb and flow of the seasons – a process of stillness, birth, activity and rest.

Once you come to fully understand your own true nature as an awakened being living out your highest purpose here on planet earth and are able to step aside to allow the flow of the universe to wash over all and everything in your organisation, then nothing will stand in the way of the great manifestation and the realisation of what might once have seemed to be an impossible dream. Add the creative power of the universe to your organisation's asset sheet and horizons of infinite possibility will open up before you.

The calling has never been stronger right now for all of us who are leaders to step into our divinity and to claim the gifts that the universe has for us. The time is right for us to extend these gifts to those that we lead, to release all of our misunderstandings and internal conflicts and blockages so that we can be an expression of the divine, of love, in the way that we lead and manage our organisations.

The imperative to wake up and grow up and to step fully into our role as a Third Level, Transcendent Leader, is a peremptory order of a most beautiful, numinous kind from the divine itself. We can make the shift and step into our highest purpose simply by saying, 'yes' to this most powerful calling. And as we do so, not only do we transform the knowledge, understanding and outcomes of those organisations that we lead, but we also contribute to the healing of the planet. All organisations on this earth, be they government departments, blue chip companies, not-for-profit organisations - they all need to experience this shift, this connection to the divine that Transcendent Leadership provides. The world needs this radical step-change in understanding more than ever at this time of great upheaval.

So unlock the foundational dimensions and then continue to loop around the cyclical dimensions and don't forget - never, ever wait until you are perfect to share your gift. The very act of opening up to the abundance of the universe will enable the great perfection to flow through you in ways that you could never have imagined.

Enjoy the ride!

We are now in a position to summarise the eighth dimension of Transcendent Leadership: Opening to stillness and presence brings energy to the cyclical dimensions of Transcendent Leadership.

Summary of Practices and Reflections in this dimension:

- Sleep Diary   225

- Schedule 'Self' Time   230

I include here a useful summary of the 8 dimensions of Transcendent Leadership:

The Foundational Dimensions:

First Dimension: Knowing (The Key to Transcendence)
Knowledge of your true nature is a necessary pre-condition and the key to becoming a Transcendent Leader.

Second Dimension: Seeing (Revealing Your Mission)
Uncovering your greatest longing and longest reach within the field of consciousness will enable you to fully see your core mission in the world.

Third Dimension: Being (Becoming You)
By consciously surrendering your egoic self, you open up to becoming one with your true nature and by so doing, shift beyond autonomic programming and create the inner conditions to become transcendent.

Fourth Dimension: Aligning (The Shift to Third Level)
The shift to Third Level leadership occurs when you align head and heart and allow your awakened state to take control of the mind, thus creating coherence within and between yourself and the organisational body.

The Cyclical Dimensions:

Fifth Dimension: Connecting (The Centrality of Love)
When you connect with your purpose and with those around you through the heart of love, you will

experience divine flow in and through you, which will preternaturally charge your leadership practice.

Sixth Dimension: Creating (Opening to Infinite Possibility)
When you tune in to the frequencies and vibration of Spirit, infinite possibility and creativity arises spontaneously and is activated in those around you via resonant transmission.

Seventh Dimension: Doing (Manifesting)
When you co-create with Spirit, abundance arises through flow. Space arises for brilliant people to be brilliant, and the team develops its own learning and growth through neuroplasticity. Through this, goals are made manifest.

Eighth Dimension: Resting (The Mind-Spirit Energy Cycle)
Opening to stillness and presence brings energy to the cyclical dimensions of Transcendent Leadership.

Postscript

Let me state briefly that in some places in the book, I have changed people's names and details such that they cannot be identified in situations where it might be inappropriate to do so.

And thus to one final point. Why me? What makes me qualified to bring you this learning? This is not an exercise in self-aggrandisement. Many authors are just that, authors. Many consultants in management have rarely managed an operational team for themselves, outside the confines of consultancy. This book presents some quite revolutionary ideas in the field of organisational leadership, and I experientially know that these techniques, whilst being a little left-field for some, actually work in practice.

This is because I continue to operate at the coal face in the world's third largest organisation, the National Health Service. What I am telling you about in this book is just about what I do every day. Following a spell in Chartered Accountancy with PWC, I pursued a career in general management in the UK, pioneering integrated systems and leadership across health and social care. I have managed up to 2,000 staff with budgets over $100 million. Latterly I have led health and care teams in a part of England that covers one of the oldest populations on the planet, with an average 40% over 65 years of age.

The outcomes that we achieved kept more people safe and well at home and away from hospital than any other area in England, as well as expediting safe discharge home faster than any other location in Devon. My teams were the most efficient in Devon, but despite achieving more through-put than any other area, they are unremittingly happy. In recognition of this unusual combination, my employer, a combined acute hospital and community health organisation, awarded me the Extraordinary Leadership Award in 2020. I had been nominated by my line reports – nurses, therapists, managers and social workers. Here are some of the comments they put forward, and again, I must emphasise that I am including them here not to show off, but to demonstrate that Transcendent Leadership really does work in the nitty-gritty of front-line management:

"Richard is a very kind/well liked manager...I have always felt supported and listened to. I have a lot of respect for a manager like Richard who recognises the importance of a happy team, and how this impacts the care that we give patients"

"Richard maintains the highest professional conduct at all times"

"Richard is enthusiastic, which rubs off on the team. He'll get out there with you, look to experience the challenges that frontline staff face. He has great awareness of what's going on in the service, reacts quickly to problems or helps to prevent problems before they happen. He empowers you to bring ideas and encourages you to ask silly questions. He recognises achievements and innovation no matter how small, and will let the staff know that he appreciates it."

"Richard has always encouraged his team to be creative and supports their diversity. He makes time for people when they are struggling or want to share successes or concerns."

"Richard's team consistently performs well"

"Richard is excellent at involving staff at all levels of decision-making. He communicates through the usual methods, however, what Richard does well that I really appreciate, is the time and effort that he will put into explaining what is going on in the service and why at face-to-face level. This is to the point where he will look for you to discuss key messages and how we may as a team, carry through the key messages. He will talk to staff at all levels and share experiences of frontline staff with managers at a higher level to inform change. He makes you feel listened to, that everyone has something to say and that we have a important role in the organisation."

"Richard is an innovator and I have no doubt that he will use any new tools and methods to enhance the performance and potentials of his team."

"It appears very strongly to me that Richard doesn't want 'yes' people in his team. He encourages independent thought and gives you the tools to develop. He has the knowledge and experience to offer expert advice when needed but on the whole uses coaching to support your development. He challenges, but in a way which helps you to look at things differently and to challenge yourself. You can always ask silly questions. If you're having a bad day and when confidence is knocked, he soaks up your negativity and you walk out feeling completely refreshed feeling good about yourself again. During hard times, even when Richard is very busy, he will seek you out to find out how you are and checking with you to see what is going on with an issue. You don't have to ask for a meeting, he will look for you."

"Richard will work with us to achieve the best outcomes for professional development and encourage us to achieve our professional goals."

"Richard builds and maintains a number of highly complex relationships with partners. He is also well regarded within the management team in which he sits."

"Richard motivates through empowerment and by acting as a most excellent role model. He appears to take great pride in the team that he leads, recognises that by taking the time out to thank people for achievements and I produced forward for well-deserved awards. He represents the ethos of the team through his compassion, client centred approach and constant drive for excellence in care. He does not just look the next few months or year, he strives for a service that he can be proud of in terms of the next 20 years. I have heard him say that he wants to leave a service that both we and the next person who comes into his role can all be proud of."

"Richard may have a facilitating/coaching style, but he also knows when to be that manager who has to take tough decisions. He will guide on policy and show me how to make painful decisions and to follow procedures when there are performance issues in the team. During such difficult times, even when Richard is very busy, he'll seek you out to find out how you are and checking with you to see what is going on within issue. Richards loves data and uses it really well to informal performance and to set benchmarks for us to work for."

"Richard demonstrates a level of knowledge beyond the norm. He may manage in a way that empowers others but he always appears to balance this with good financial and business planning. He has great knowledge of legal, ethical and policy side of health and social care which he shares and ensures is followed."

"Richard is the data King!"

"Richard delegates whilst at the same time he can be protective. I can tell when he recognises that maybe I am getting out of my depth. He shows understanding and empathy and will step in to offer advice and talk through something rather than watching me struggle. He doesn't leave it there. He will then point me in the right direction to enable me to be able to learn and become competent."

"Richard encourages us all to be creative and work things out for ourselves to benefit the people in our care."

"Richard is a strong and enthusiastic leader of change. He leads from the front, and leaves no stone unturned and will involve all staff at every stage of the change process. Richard can be relied upon to do his bits and works tirelessly to ensure that the reason for the change and possible benefits are understood."

"It is very obvious from the way Richard works that he really is people-focused. He ensures that not only is the business fit for the purpose it's meant for but also that it is patient-centred. He will always question "Have you thought about this from the patient's / relatives / carers view?" it's not just about hitting targets and agendas.

"We are lucky in the team to have Richard, he inspires us all to be better constantly and always look to improve services for those patients that we look after."

Here are some things that coaching clients have said:

"Richard met my hopes and wishes for growth with confidence and kindness right away, which gave me a lot of self-belief. Working with him in coaching was a deep and transformative experience, with lots of layers and shifts occurring, and always beautifully framed in a professional and practical plan.
I began in a place of lack and powerlessness I didn't even really notice I was in, and by the end had ideas for my own future, and belief I could reach them for the first time. It was subtle and gentle, but a big change.
Richard is an inspiring and supportive coach. I felt just challenged enough and just supported enough to really let my own strength come into awareness, and be willing to share it. I notice changes in my thoughts and behaviours now, I am braver, and more determined to share whatever I have with the world - and I know what that is! It was a wonderful experience that I'm really glad I had."

"Richard, I now have a different energy and mind-set. I've come such a long way. I've learnt a lot about happiness. It's core to how I feel right now. I don't now feel any external pressure. I don't now feel the need to achieve things to feel deeply fulfilled in myself. I feel mentally much healthier. I feel I know how to be myself now. What you've done is helped to channel the real me into my life. The meditative processes are just brilliant in the sessions.

I have changed my mind-set beyond belief. I'm thrilled. I now have the mind-set that all things are possible. Even some of my original goals have resolved as I now see the world through a new lens. Brilliant and amazing!"

"Richard, my brother. I just wanted to say thank you. You cannot buy what you gave me this morning."

"Richard is the real deal. He's smart, authentic and heartfelt. He connected with me quickly and helped me to overcome procrastination, doubt and playing safe. In a short series of powerful, fun and light-hearted sessions, Richard believed in me, inspired me, uplifted me, and loved me through my self sabotage, doubt and fear. I feel like I've finally crossed a bridge in my life I'd been walking for quite a while. I'd work with him again with pleasure!"

"You know in this technological world we now inhabit one often reads or hears advertisements about powering into the future, powering into tomorrow, however if one is really interested into powering or changing their forward momentum, then their passion is in advancing in a direction their consciousness hasn't embraced yet. It's really realizing where you have been, hasn't gotten, what you feel you want; it's this realization that is the key. From here the go to person is Richard Anderson as he is excellent in bringing you into this instant. This instant is really all we really have, everything is life flows forward from this instant. Forget about words like powering and change which emphasize duality and instead, working with Richard you will learn what embodying this instant is and as you do a different person emerges."

www.ingramcontent.com/pod-product-compliance
Lightning Source LLC
Chambersburg PA
CBHW070620220526
45466CB00001B/65